WE GOT
LEADERSHIP
WRONG

*The Reality of Leadership for
Business and Human Sustainability*

Fahad Khalaf aka Coach Fahad

CONTENTS

INTRODUCTION

Leadership has been a topic of discussion for as long as humans have organised themselves into groups. Throughout history, leaders have been seen as figures who command respect and wield power, shaping the course of events and determining the fate of nations. However, in recent years, a growing number of experts have begun to question whether our understanding of leadership is still relevant in the modern world.

Traditionally, leadership has been seen as a hierarchical and top-down process. Leaders were expected to set the direction, make the decisions, and ensure that their followers executed their plans. This model was appropriate for a world in which information flowed from the top to the bottom, and change was relatively slow. However, in the rapidly changing world of the 21st century, this model is increasingly inadequate.

In today's complex and interconnected world, leaders must be able to navigate through uncertainty and ambiguity. They must be able to adapt to changing circumstances and engage with stakeholders in new and creative ways. They must be able to lead in a world where the traditional sources of power and authority are being challenged and where the flow of information is no longer one-way, from the top to the bottom.

To meet these challenges, a growing number of experts have begun to explore alternative models of leadership. One of the most promising models is collaborative leadership, which recognises the importance of engaging and empowering individuals and teams. Collaborative leaders work to build relationships, foster collaboration, and create a shared vision of the future. They recognise that their role is not simply to dictate but to facilitate and support their followers in achieving their goals.

Another model that has gained recognition in recent years is servant leadership. Servant leaders put the needs of others first, using their power and influence to help them achieve their goals. They recognise that leadership is not just about achieving their own objectives but about creating a better world for everyone. By focusing on the needs of others, servant leaders are able to build trust and engagement, creating a culture of collaboration and teamwork.

These alternative models of leadership are not without their limitations, however. Collaborative leadership can sometimes be too focused on consensus, making it difficult to make tough decisions. Servant leadership can also be challenging, as it requires leaders to sacrifice their own interests for the benefit of others. Nevertheless, these models offer a fresh perspective on leadership and provide a framework for leaders to navigate through the challenges of the modern world.

Our understanding of leadership has changed dramatically in recent years. The traditional top-down model of leadership is no longer adequate in a world of complexity and uncertainty. Alternative models, such as collaborative and servant leadership, offer a more nuanced understanding of leadership and provide leaders with the tools they need to succeed in the 21st century. Whether we have "gotten leadership wrong" in the past is a matter of debate, but it is certain that the way we lead and the way we think about leadership are changing. Therefore, leaders who embrace this change will be best equipped to lead their organisations and communities into the future.

PART-1

WHAT PEOPLE ARE GETTING WRONG WITH LEADERSHIP

One of the key things that people are getting wrong about leadership is their assumption that the traditional top-down model of leadership is still appropriate in today's rapidly changing and complex world. This model, which assumes that leaders set the direction and make the decisions, is based on a hierarchical and centralised approach to leadership. However, in a world of rapid change and increasing complexity, this model is increasingly inadequate.

Another aspect of leadership that people are getting wrong is their belief that leadership is solely about having power and authority. While power and authority are both important, they are not the only factors that determine leadership success. In today's world, leaders must also be able to engage and empower individuals and teams, build relationships, and foster collaboration. They must be able to navigate through uncertainty and ambiguity and adapt to changing circumstances. These skills and qualities are just as important as power and authority in determining leadership success.

A third aspect of leadership that people are getting wrong is their idea that leadership is a one-size-fits-all approach. The reality is that there is no single model of leadership that works in all situations. Different models are appropriate for different contexts, and leaders must be able to adapt their approach to the situation at hand. For example, in some situations, a hierarchical and top-down approach may be appropriate, while in others, a collaborative and servant approach may be more effective. Leaders must be able to recognise the different contexts and adjust their approach accordingly.

Finally, people are often getting wrong their idea that leadership is an individual trait. While individual leaders do play a critical role in shaping the direction of organisations and communities, leadership is not just about the actions of individual leaders. It is also about the relationships and interactions that take place within organisations and communities. Effective leadership requires the engagement and participation of individuals and teams, and leaders must be able to facilitate and support these relationships if they are to be successful.

In summary, there are many things that people are getting wrong about leadership in today's rapidly changing world. The traditional top-down model of leadership is no longer adequate, and leaders must be able to adapt their approach to the different situations at hand. They must also recognise that leadership is not just about having power and authority, but it is about engaging and empowering individuals and teams. Effective leadership requires the participation of everyone, and leaders must be able to facilitate and support the relationships and interactions that take place within organisations and communities. By understanding these key aspects of leadership, leaders can be better equipped to navigate through the challenges of the modern world and also lead their organisations and communities into the future.

PART-2

TRADITIONAL PERSPECTIVES OF LEADERSHIP

The study of leadership has been an ongoing pursuit for centuries, and various traditional perspectives on leadership have been developed over time. Here's a detailed explanation of each of the six traditional perspectives on leadership:

Trait Theory: This perspective argues that leaders possess certain inherent traits or characteristics that make them effective. Proponents of this theory believe that leaders are born with certain qualities, such as intelligence, charisma, determination, and confidence, which enable them to lead others successfully. Researchers have attempted to identify the specific traits that distinguish leaders from non-leaders, but there is still much debate over which traits are most critical to effective leadership.

Behavioural Theory: This perspective focuses on the observable actions or behaviours of leaders and argues that effective leadership is based on specific behaviours rather than inherent traits. According to this theory, leaders who exhibit certain behaviours, such as being directive, supportive, and participative, are more effective leaders than those who do not exhibit such behaviours. The behavioural approach to leadership identifies specific behaviours that can be taught and learned, which makes it a useful tool for developing leadership skills.

Contingency Theory: This perspective asserts that there is no one-size-fits-all approach to leadership and that the most effective leadership style depends on the situation at hand. According to the contingency theory, different situations call for different leadership styles, and the leader must therefore adapt their style to the particular demands of each situation. For example, in a crisis situation, a directive leadership style may be more effective, while in a stable and predictable environment, a supportive or participative style may be more appropriate.

Situational Theory: This perspective is similar to the contingency theory, and it emphasises the importance of adapting leadership styles to the specific demands of the situation. According to the situational theory, the most effective leadership style depends on the readiness or ability of the followers to accept and implement change. This implies that a leader who is able to assess the readiness of their followers and adjust their style accordingly is more likely to be effective.

Path-Goal Theory: This theory suggests that leaders can influence the motivation and satisfaction of their followers by clarifying their path to attain desired goals and removing obstacles. Here, the leader's role is to help their followers understand how their efforts contribute to the achievement of organisational goals and to provide them with the necessary support and resources to overcome obstacles. According to the path-goal theory, the leader's style should be adapted to meet the needs and expectations of their followers in a given situation.

Transformational Theory: This perspective views leadership as a process of inspiring and empowering followers to achieve a shared vision. According to the transformational theory, leaders who are able to articulate a compelling vision and inspire their followers to work towards its attainment are more likely to be effective. The transformational leader motivates and inspires his/her followers by appealing to their values, beliefs, and aspirations and by creating a sense of community and shared purpose.

Each of these traditional perspectives provides valuable insights into the nature of leadership, and by combining and integrating elements of each perspective, we can develop a more comprehensive and nuanced understanding of leadership.

PART-3

TRADITIONAL TRAITS OF LEADERSHIP

The trait theory of leadership is a traditional perspective that posits that effective leaders possess certain inherent traits or characteristics that distinguish them from non-leaders. This theory is based on the belief that some individuals are born with qualities that make them better suited to lead others, while others may never develop these qualities no matter how hard they try.

The theory is rooted in the idea that leadership is an innate quality and that certain individuals are born with the natural ability to lead. Proponents of the trait theory believe that these individuals possess certain traits that make them effective leaders, such as intelligence, charisma, confidence, determination, emotional stability, honesty, and integrity. These traits are often viewed as being essential to effective leadership, as they allow leaders to inspire and motivate their followers, make decisions and take action, and earn the trust and respect of their followers.

While the trait theory of leadership has been widely studied, there is still much debate over which traits are most critical to effective leadership and whether leaders are born with these traits or can develop them over time. Some researchers also argue that some of the traits commonly associated with effective leadership, such as intelligence and emotional stability, are innate traits that cannot be learned, while others believe that these traits can be developed and honed through training and experience.

Despite these debates, the trait theory of leadership continues to be an important and influential perspective on the nature of leadership. By focusing on the traits and characteristics of leaders, the trait theory provides a framework for understanding what qualities and abilities make someone an effective leader. This understanding can be useful in developing leadership training programs, selecting and promoting leaders, and creating leadership development initiatives.

While the trait theory of leadership has its limitations, it remains an important and enduring perspective on the nature of leadership. By focusing on the inherent traits and characteristics of leaders, it provides valuable insights into what makes some individuals more effective at leading others than others.

Psychometric assessments and tools have become increasingly popular in recent years for evaluating the leadership potential of individuals. These assessments are designed to measure various personality traits, cognitive abilities, and behavioural patterns that are believed to be indicative of effective leadership. The premise behind these assessments is that by identifying an individual's strengths and weaknesses, organisations can then better match them with their right leadership roles.

However, there is still an ongoing debate about the validity and effectiveness of these psychometric assessments in determining traditional traits of leadership. On one hand, proponents argue that these assessments provide valuable insights into an individual's strengths and weaknesses and can help organisations make informed decisions about promotions and assignments. They also highlight the importance of considering personality traits, such as emotional intelligence and adaptability, that are believed to be critical for effective leadership.

On the other hand, opponents argue that psychometric assessments are limited in their ability to predict leadership success. They point out that these assessments only measure a limited set of traits and may not accurately reflect an individual's potential for leadership. Additionally, these assessments can also be biased towards certain personality traits or cultural norms and may overlook important skills and abilities that are also critical for effective leadership.

Despite these debates, there is evidence to suggest that psychometric assessments can be useful tools for organisations in determining leadership potential. For example, studies have shown that emotional intelligence, which is often measured by these assessments, is positively correlated with leadership effectiveness. Additionally, research has also shown that cognitive abilities, such as problem-solving and decision-making skills, can also be predictive of leadership success.

Psychometric assessments and tools have been widely used in evaluating and predicting leadership traits, but they have faced a lot of criticism in recent years. One of the main areas where these assessments failed is in their limited scope of measurement. While they can provide valuable insight into a person's cognitive abilities, personality, and behaviour, they do not always accurately reflect their leadership potential.

Another issue is that these assessments can be subjective and may not take into account the context and culture in which the individual operates. For example, a person who scores well on a psychometric assessment may not necessarily be an effective leader in a different organisational culture or context.

Additionally, the results of these assessments can be easily influenced by the individual's level of self-awareness and self-reflection, as well as the potential for bias in the interpretation of the results.

Moreover, psychometric assessments and tools also rely heavily on past behaviour and experiences, which can be misleading in predicting the future behaviour and performance as a leader. This is because leadership is a dynamic and evolving process that can be impacted by numerous external and internal factors, such as changes in the market, organisational structure, and personal growth and development.

While these psychometric assessments can be useful tools for organisations in determining the traditional traits of leadership, it is important to approach them with caution and also consider their limitations. Organisations should not rely solely on these assessments when making decisions about leadership potential, but they should also consider other factors such as experience, skills, and behaviour. Ultimately, the effectiveness of psychometric assessments will depend on how they are used and the interpretation of the results.

PART-4

LEADERSHIP FAILURES

L eadership is both a complex and challenging task that requires a combination of skills, abilities, and personality traits. Despite the best intentions and efforts of many leaders, many of them still fail in their leadership roles. Understanding the reasons why individuals may fail in leadership is essential for improving leadership effectiveness and avoiding common pitfalls.

There are many reasons why individuals may fail in leadership, and these reasons can be broadly categorised into lack of vision, ineffective communication, lack of emotional intelligence, inadequate decision-making skills, resistance to change, lack of trust, poor delegation skills, and an inability to inspire and motivate others. These factors can interact and compound to create leadership failure, and they can have serious consequences for the leader, their organisation, and the people they serve.

First of all, leaders who lack a clear vision for their organisation can struggle to inspire and motivate their followers. Without a clear direction and purpose, followers may become disillusioned and disengaged, making it difficult for the leader to achieve their goals. If the leader also lacks effective communication skills, they may struggle to articulate their vision and goals to their followers, further undermining their ability to lead effectively. Effective communication is critical for leaders, as it allows them to articulate their vision, goals, and expectations and to engage and inspire their followers.

Leaders who lack emotional intelligence may struggle to manage their own emotions and the emotions of others, which can lead to conflicts and poor morale. This can also impact their decision-making ability, as emotions can cloud judgement and lead to poor decision-making. Emotional intelligence is a critical component of effective leadership, as it allows leaders to understand and manage their own emotions and the emotions of others and create a positive and supportive work environment.

Leaders who are unwilling or unable to adapt to changing circumstances and embrace new ideas may also struggle to lead effectively. They may resist change and become entrenched in their own ways, failing to recognise the need for growth and adaptation in their organisation. In today's rapidly changing world, it is essential for leaders to be flexible and adaptable and to embrace new ideas and approaches that can improve their organisation and benefit their followers.

Lack of trust is another common reason for leadership failure. Leaders who lack the trust of their followers are less likely to be effective, as trust is a critical component of effective leadership. Trust allows leaders to establish credibility and build relationships with their followers, which is essential for inspiring and motivating them. Trust can be built over time through consistent and transparent behaviour, but it can be quickly eroded through dishonesty or unethical behaviour.

Poor delegation skills can also lead to leadership failure. Leaders who are unable to delegate responsibilities effectively can become overwhelmed and struggle to lead their organisations effectively. Effective delegation allows leaders to distribute tasks and responsibilities among their team members, freeing up their time and energy to focus on more important tasks and initiatives. However, poor delegation skills can lead to failure in effectively managing tasks and responsibilities and can ultimately result in burnout and disengagement among team members.

Finally, leaders who lack the ability to inspire and motivate their followers are less likely to be successful, as effective leadership requires the ability to inspire and motivate others. Inspiring and motivating followers requires a deeper understanding of their motivations and needs, as well as the ability to communicate and connect with them in meaningful ways. Leaders who are unable to inspire and motivate their followers are less likely to achieve their goals and are more likely to fail in their leadership role. There are many reasons why people may fail in leadership positions, and it is essential for leaders to be self-reflective and open to constructive feedback in order to continuously improve upon their skills and abilities and minimise the risk of failure. By understanding the common reasons for leadership failure, leaders can take steps to avoid it.

EXAMPLE:

A CEO of a large corporation lacked a clear vision for the company and was unable to effectively communicate that vision to his employees. This lack of direction and poor communication decreased morale and engagement among employees, as they felt uninspired and disconnected from the company's goals. The CEO also struggled with emotional intelligence, frequently lashing out at employees and creating a toxic work environment. This lack of emotional intelligence, combined with resistance to change, as the CEO was unwilling to embrace new ideas and adapt to changing market conditions, led to poor decision-making and a decline in the company's performance.

The CEO also struggled with trust, as employees felt that he was not transparent or honest in his communication with them. This lack of trust eroded the CEO's credibility and made it difficult for him to lead effectively. Additionally, the CEO had poor delegation skills, frequently micromanaging employees and becoming overwhelmed with tasks and responsibilities. Finally, the CEO lacked the ability to inspire and motivate his employees and was unable to create a positive and supportive work environment that would enable his employees to reach their full potential.

As a result of these factors, the CEO ultimately failed in his leadership role, and the company's performance suffered. In order to avoid similar failures in leadership, it is essential for leaders to understand the importance of vision, communication, emotional intelligence, decision-making, flexibility, trust, delegation, and the ability to inspire and motivate others.

PART-5

DIFFERENCE BETWEEN A GOOD LEADER AND A BAD LEADER

Leadership is a critical component of organisational success, and the difference between a good leader and a bad leader can have significant impacts on the success of an organisation. A good leader is someone who inspires, motivates, and guides their team toward achieving common goals, while a bad leader creates confusion, undermines morale, and causes harm to the organisation.

Here are some of the key differences between a good leader and a bad leader:

Vision: A good leader has a clear and inspiring vision for their organisation and is able to effectively communicate that vision to others. They inspire their team to work together towards a common goal, and their vision serves as a guiding principle for the organisation. A bad leader, on the other hand, lacks direction and fails to communicate effectively. They may not have a clear vision for the organisation, or if they do, they are unable to communicate it effectively to their team. This lack of direction creates confusion and undermines morale, as employees are unsure of the organisation's goals and objectives.

Emotional Intelligence: Good leaders have high emotional intelligence and are able to understand and manage their own emotions and those of their followers. They create a positive and supportive work environment and are able to resolve conflicts and build strong relationships with their team. Bad leaders, on the other hand, struggle with emotional regulation and may create a toxic work environment. They may lash out at employees, undermine morale, and cause harm to the organisation through their own actions and behaviour.

Decision-Making: Good leaders make well-informed and ethical decisions that are in the best interest of their organisation. They weigh the potential outcomes of their decisions and make choices that are aligned with the organisation's values and goals. Bad leaders, on the other hand, make hasty or unethical decisions that may harm the organisation. They may prioritise their own interests over those of the organisation or make decisions without considering the potential consequences.

Flexibility: Good leaders are adaptable and open to change. They recognise that the business environment is constantly changing, and they are able to adjust their approach and strategies to meet new challenges and opportunities. Bad leaders resist change and struggle to adjust to new circumstances. They may cling to outdated strategies and approaches, even when they are no longer effective, and may be unwilling to embrace new ideas and perspectives.

Trust: Good leaders are transparent and build trust with their employees. They are honest and open in their communication, and they create a culture of trust within their organisation. This trust enables employees to feel confident and comfortable in their work, and it fosters collaboration and teamwork. Bad leaders erode trust through dishonesty or lack of transparency. They may hide information from employees or communicate to employees in a way that undermines trust, causing harm to the organisation.

Delegation: Good leaders delegate tasks effectively, thereby empowering employees to reach their full potential. They trust their team to handle tasks and responsibilities, and they provide support and guidance as needed. Bad leaders micromanage or become overwhelmed with tasks and responsibilities. They may take on too much work, or they may interfere with their team's work and undermine their ability to perform effectively.

Inspiration: Good leaders inspire and motivate their employees to reach their full potential. They create a positive and supportive work environment that enables employees to grow and develop. Good leaders also recognise and reward employee achievements. Bad leaders fail to create a positive and supportive work environment, and they may undermine morale and cause harm to the organisation.

In conclusion, good leaders have a clear vision, high emotional intelligence, make ethical decisions, are adaptable, build trust, delegate effectively, and inspire and motivate others. They create a positive and supportive work environment that enables employees to reach their full potential, and they lead their organisation toward success.

PART-6

DIFFERENCE BETWEEN A GOOD PERSONALITY AND A BAD PERSONALITY

The distinction between a good personality and a bad personality is very important, as our personality influences the way we interact with others, how we approach life, and the kind of impact we have on the people and the world around us.

A good personality is often characterised by traits such as empathy, kindness, generosity, honesty, integrity, and a positive attitude. People with good personalities are often well-liked, respected, and admired by those around them. They have the ability to build strong relationships, resolve conflicts, and maintain healthy boundaries in their personal and professional lives. A good personality can also have a positive impact on our well-being and happiness, as well as the well-being and happiness of those around us.

Empathy is an important trait of a good personality. Empathy is the ability to understand and share the feelings of others. People with good personalities are often able to put themselves in other people's shoes, and they are able to understand and show compassion and kindness toward others. This makes them effective communicators and problem solvers, as they are able to understand the perspectives of those around them.

Kindness and generosity are also important traits of a good personality. People with good personalities are often known for their kindness, compassion, and willingness to help others. They are willing to offer themselves and their resources to those in need, and they often put the needs of others before their own. This creates a positive environment, as those around them feel valued and supported.

Honesty and integrity are also key traits of a good personality. People with good personalities are often known for their honesty and straightforwardness, and they are trusted by those around them. They are committed to doing the right thing, even when it may not be the easiest or most convenient choice. This builds trust and respect in relationships, and it creates a foundation for open and honest communication.

Finally, a positive attitude is an important aspect of a good personality. People with good personalities tend to have a positive outlook on life, and they are able to maintain this positive attitude even in the face of adversity. They are often energetic, optimistic, and supportive, and they bring a sense of positivity and light to those around them.

On the other hand, a bad personality is characterised by traits such as selfishness, cruelty, dishonesty, arrogance, and a negative attitude. People with bad personalities may engage in harmful behaviours, cause harm to others, and have difficulty building and maintaining relationships. They may also have difficulty resolving conflicts and may struggle with personal and professional boundaries. A bad personality can have a negative impact on our well-being and happiness, as well as the well-being and happiness of those around us.

Selfishness is a common trait of a bad personality. People with bad personalities may put their own needs and wants ahead of the needs and wants of others. This can lead to a behaviour that is harmful to others, as they prioritise their own interests over the interests of others. This can create conflict and tension in relationships, as others feel disregarded and disrespected.

Cruelty is another trait of a bad personality. People with bad personalities may engage in behaviours that are intentionally hurtful or harmful to others. This may take the form of physical or emotional abuse, or it may take the form of intentional neglect or disregard. This type of behaviour creates a negative environment, and it can have a lasting impact on the well-being and happiness of those who are subjected to it.

Dishonesty and a lack of integrity are also traits of a bad personality. People with bad personalities may be known for their dishonesty and untrustworthiness. They may engage in behaviours that are deceptive or manipulative, and they may not be committed.

PART-7

ROLE OF A LEADER AT AN ORGANISATION

The role of a leader in an organisation is crucial to the success of the organisation. Leaders play a key role in setting the direction, establishing the culture, and guiding the performance of their team or organisation. A leader's role includes setting and communicating the vision, inspiring and motivating others, making decisions, and developing and implementing strategies.

Vision and strategy: First of all, a leader's role is to create a vision for the organisation and to develop and implement strategies that will help the organisation achieve its goals. Leaders must be able to see the big picture, identify trends and opportunities, and set a clear direction for the organisation. They must be able to articulate this vision into the organisation and inspire and motivate others to work towards achieving it. Leaders also must be able to develop and implement effective strategies that align with the organisation's vision, values, and goals.

Inspiring and motivating others: A leader's role is to inspire and motivate others to achieve the organisation's goals. Leaders must be able to communicate their vision and strategies effectively and create a culture of performance and accountability. They must also be able to recognise and reward individual and team performance and create an environment that encourages innovation and continuous improvement.

Making decisions: A leader's role is to make informed and effective decisions that impact the organisation. Leaders must be able to gather information, analyse data, and make informed decisions based on what is best for the organisation. They must also be able to balance the needs of the organisation with the needs of their team and individuals. Leaders must be able to make decisions in a timely manner and take responsibility for their decisions.

Developing and managing relationships: A leader's role is to develop and manage relationships with stakeholders, including employees, customers, suppliers, and shareholders. Leaders must be able to communicate effectively with all stakeholders and create and maintain a positive working environment for employees. Leaders must also be able to build and manage relationships with key stakeholders and work collaboratively with other organisations and leaders.

Developing talent: A leader's role is to develop the talent of their team and the organisation. Leaders must be able to identify the strengths and weaknesses of their team and provide opportunities for their growth and development. Leaders must also be able to create a culture that encourages and supports learning, innovation, and continuous improvement.

The role of a leader in an organisation is both complex and multifaceted. Leaders play a critical role in setting the direction, establishing the culture, and guiding the performance of their team or organisation. To be effective, leaders must possess a combination of technical skills, knowledge, and leadership abilities. They must be able to communicate effectively, inspire and motivate others, make informed decisions, and develop and manage relationships. Ultimately, the role of a leader in an organisation is to create a vision, develop and implement strategies, and inspire and motivate others to achieve the organisation's goals.

Developing a clear and compelling vision is a crucial aspect of effective leadership. A strong vision can inspire and motivate employees, drive innovation, and steer the organization towards success. However, developing a vision and embodying visionary leadership is not an easy task. It requires a leader to be forward-thinking, innovative, and strategic in their approach. In this section, we will discuss the step-by-step process of how to develop vision and visionary leadership in an organization.

Step 1: Self-reflection: The first step in developing a vision and visionary leadership is self-reflection. A leader must take the time to reflect on their values, strengths, and weaknesses. Self-reflection helps a leader identify their passion, purpose, and direction in life. A clear understanding of oneself helps in creating a more authentic and credible vision.

Step 2: Understand the organization's current state: The second step in developing a vision is understanding the current state of the organization. This includes analyzing the organization's strengths, weaknesses, opportunities, and threats (SWOT analysis). Understanding the current state of the organization helps in identifying gaps and opportunities for improvement.

Step 3: Define the future state: Once a leader has a clear understanding of the current state of the organization, they can define the future state. This is the desired state the organization should aim to achieve. A leader should create a clear and concise vision statement that outlines the future state of the organization.

Step 4: Communicate the vision: After defining the future state, the leader must communicate the vision to the organization. A leader should ensure that the vision is clear, concise, and easy to understand. Communication should be done through various channels such as town hall meetings, email, and social media. A leader should also ensure that employees understand the benefits of achieving the vision.

Step 5: Align the organization: The next step is to align the organization to the vision. A leader should create a plan of action that outlines how the organization will achieve the vision. This includes identifying the necessary resources, setting goals, and creating a timeline. A leader should also ensure that employees understand their roles in achieving the vision and how their work contributes to the organization's success.

To be more technical, a clear vision serves as a roadmap, guiding decisions and actions towards a common goal. A leader who can effectively establish and articulate a vision for the future can inspire their team to greatness and propel the organization forward. In this section, we will explore the steps to developing a good vision for an organization.

Step 1: Conduct a Visioning Session

The first step in developing a vision for an organization is conducting a visioning session. This session should be an inclusive process that involves key stakeholders, including employees, customers, and other relevant parties. The goal of this session is to identify what the organization wants to achieve in the long-term, usually over a period of 5 to 10 years. The facilitator of the session should encourage participants to think creatively and expansively, asking questions like "How would the organization look if it was the best in the world at what it does?" and "What new markets or products could the organization pursue?"

Step 2: Identify Core Values

Once the vision has been identified, the next step is to identify the core values that underpin it. Core values are the beliefs and principles that guide the organization's behavior, and they should be reflected in everything that the organization does. Examples of core values might include integrity, innovation, customer service, or teamwork. Once these values have been identified, they should be communicated throughout the organization, and leaders should model them in their own behavior.

Step 3: Communicate the Vision

After the vision and core values have been identified, the next step is to communicate them throughout the organization. This is a critical step in the process, as employees need to comprehend and buy into the vision for it to be successful.

Leaders should be clear and consistent in their communication, explaining the vision in simple terms and highlighting how each employee's work contributes to the larger goal.

Step 4: Develop Action Plans

Once the vision has been communicated, the next step is to develop action plans to achieve it. These action plans should be developed collaboratively, with input from all relevant parties. Each action plan should be aligned with the vision and core values, and should include specific objectives, timelines, and metrics for success. Regular progress updates should be communicated throughout the organization, highlighting successes and challenges along the way. Here are a few things to consider while developing a good vision for your company:

Define the purpose and values: Developing a vision for the organization requires a clear understanding of the organization's purpose and values. The purpose defines the organization's reason for existence, and the values define its principles and beliefs. By defining purpose and values, the organization can create a foundation for the vision.

Conduct a SWOT analysis: A SWOT analysis is a tool that helps identify the organization's strengths, weaknesses, opportunities, and threats. By conducting a SWOT analysis, the organization can gain a better understanding of its current position and potential future scenarios, which can help inform the vision.

Envision the future: A good vision should be future-oriented, which means it should describe a desirable future state for the organization. The vision should be aspirational and challenging, yet achievable. It should also align with the purpose and values of the organization.

Engage stakeholders: Developing a vision should be a collaborative process that involves stakeholders from all levels of the organization. Engaging stakeholders can help ensure that the vision is grounded in the organization's reality and reflects the aspirations of its members.

Communicate the vision: Once the vision is developed, it is essential to communicate it effectively to all stakeholders. The communication should be clear, concise, and compelling, and it should inspire people to take action.

Align strategies and actions: A good vision should guide the organization's strategies and actions. It should be integrated into the organization's planning and decision-making processes, and it should serve as a reference point for all activities.

Measure progress: A vision should not be static; rather it should evolve as the organization progresses. To ensure that the organization is moving in the right direction, it is essential to measure progress against the vision regularly.

Foster a culture of innovation: A good vision should encourage innovation and creativity, and it should foster a culture that values experimentation and risk-taking. This can help the organization adapt to changing circumstances and stay ahead of the competition.

Lead by example: Finally, developing a good vision requires visionary leadership. Leaders must set a good example and embody the vision's values and principles. They must also be willing to take risks and make bold decisions that align with the vision.

Step 5: Evaluate Progress

The final step in developing a vision for an organization is evaluating progress regularly. This involves measuring progress against the objectives and metrics identified in the action plans, and making adjustments as needed. Leaders should be open to receiving feedback and be willing to make changes to the vision or action plans as needed, in response to the organization's evolving needs and challenges.

How to measure a good vision at a company?

A good vision is an essential element of effective leadership in any organization. It acts as a guiding light and inspires employees to work towards a common goal. However, it is not enough to just have a vision. Leaders must also be able to measure and evaluate the effectiveness of their vision to ensure that it is leading the organization in the right direction. In this section, we will discuss how to measure a good vision at an organization and how to ensure that the vision is sound.

First and foremost, a good vision must be clear and concise. It should clearly state the organization's purpose, values, and goals in a way that is easy to understand and communicate. A clear vision is critical to ensuring that all employees understand the organization's direction and their role in achieving its goals. To measure the clarity of the vision, leaders can conduct surveys or focus groups to get feedback from employees. The results can help identify areas that may need improvement or clarification.

Another critical factor in measuring the effectiveness of a vision is to evaluate whether the vision aligns with the organization's values and mission. A vision that is not in alignment with the organization's values and mission is unlikely to be effective. To ensure that the vision is in alignment with the organization's values and mission, leaders must communicate the vision to all employees and encourage feedback. They must also continuously monitor the vision to ensure that it remains relevant and aligned with the organization's values and mission.

A good vision should also be motivating and inspiring. It should excite and inspire employees to work towards achieving the organization's goals. To measure the motivating and inspiring nature of the vision, leaders can monitor employee engagement levels, conduct surveys or focus groups, and regularly communicate the vision to all employees. Leaders can also share success stories that illustrate how the vision has helped the organization achieve its goals.

The success of a vision also depends on its practicality and achievability. Leaders must ensure that the vision is realistic and can be achieved within the organization's resources and capabilities. To measure the practicality of the vision, leaders must regularly evaluate the progress made towards achieving the vision's goals. If progress is slow or non-existent, leaders must re-evaluate the vision and make any necessary adjustments.

Finally, a good vision must be adaptable and flexible. In today's rapidly evolving business environment, leaders must be able to adapt and adjust their vision to changing circumstances. A vision that is too rigid or inflexible is unlikely to be successful. To measure the adaptability of the vision, leaders must regularly evaluate the external environment and make any necessary adjustments to the vision.

One way to measure the effectiveness of a vision is by using key performance indicators (KPIs) that are aligned with the vision. For example, if the vision is to increase market share by 10% in the next year, then KPIs related to market share such as customer acquisition rate, customer retention rate, and sales growth rate can be tracked and analyzed to determine if the vision is being achieved.

Another way to measure the effectiveness of a vision is through feedback from stakeholders such as employees, customers, and shareholders. Regular surveys, focus groups, and town hall meetings can be conducted to gather feedback on the vision and its implementation. This feedback can be used to make adjustments to the vision as needed and to ensure that it remains relevant and aligned with the organization's goals.

In addition, it is important to consider the clarity and specificity of the vision. A good vision should be clear, concise, and easy to understand. It should also be specific enough to provide guidance and direction for the organization, but not so specific that it limits creativity and innovation.

The effectiveness of a vision can be measured by its impact on the organization's culture and values. A good vision should inspire and motivate employees to work towards a common goal, and should align with the organization's values and principles. If the vision is not aligned with the organization's culture and values, it may be difficult to achieve and sustain over the long term.

Measuring the effectiveness of a vision requires a combination of quantitative and qualitative methods, as well as ongoing assessment and refinement to ensure that it remains relevant and aligned with the organization's goals and values.

In summary, developing a good vision and measuring its effectiveness is critical to effective leadership. To measure a good vision, leaders must evaluate its clarity, alignment with the organization's values and mission, motivating and inspiring nature, practicality and achievability, and adaptability and flexibility. Leaders must continuously monitor and adjust the vision to ensure that it remains relevant and effective in guiding the organization towards its goals.

PART-8

CONNECTION BETWEEN LEADERSHIP AND TECHNICAL EXPERTISE

Leadership and technical expertise are two critical components of success in many industries, and they are often interconnected. In order to be an effective leader, one must possess both technical knowledge and skills, as well as leadership skills and abilities.

From a technical perspective, having a deeper understanding of one's area of expertise is crucial for success. This includes having a solid understanding of industry-specific technologies, processes, and methodologies. Technical experts have the ability to identify problems, evaluate solutions, and make informed decisions based on their knowledge and experience. They are also able to effectively communicate complex technical concepts to others and translate technical information into actionable insights.

Having a strong technical background can also help leaders to gain the respect and trust of their employees. When a leader understands the details of their work, they are better able to make informed decisions, communicate effectively with their team, and understand the challenges they face. This knowledge and expertise also allow leaders to provide guidance and support to their teams and make informed decisions about the direction of their projects and initiatives.

In addition to technical knowledge and skills, effective leaders also possess strong leadership skills. This includes the ability to inspire, motivate, and engage their team. Good leaders are able to set clear goals and objectives and communicate these goals effectively to their teams. They are able to create a positive work environment and foster a culture of collaboration and teamwork. They are able to make decisions quickly and effectively and take calculated risks when necessary.

Leadership also requires the ability to delegate and empower others. Good leaders are able to identify the strengths of their team members and assign tasks and responsibilities accordingly. They are able to delegate effectively while also ensuring that their team members have the necessary support and resources to succeed. This empowers team members to take ownership of their work, and it allows leaders to focus on other important tasks and responsibilities.

In summary, effective leadership and technical expertise are both critical components of success in many industries. Having a strong technical background allows leaders to make informed decisions, communicate effectively with their team, and understand the challenges they face. In turn, strong leadership skills allow leaders to inspire, motivate, and engage their team and create a positive work environment that fosters collaboration and teamwork. Ultimately, the connection between leadership and technical expertise is a symbiotic one, and the combination of these two skills allows individuals to achieve great success in their careers.

EXAMPLE:

A good example of the connection between leadership and technical expertise can be seen in the technology industry. Consider a project manager at a software development company who is responsible for leading a team of developers. In order to be successful in this role, the project manager must possess both technical knowledge and skills, as well as leadership abilities.

From a technical perspective, the project manager must have a deeper understanding of software development processes and methodologies. He/she must be familiar with various programming languages, software development tools, and the latest industry trends. This technical knowledge allows the project manager to communicate effectively with the development team and understand the challenges they face.

In addition to technical expertise, the project manager must also possess strong leadership skills. He/she must be able to set clear goals and objectives and communicate these goals effectively to the development team. He/she must also be able to create a positive work environment and foster a culture of collaboration and teamwork. Additionally, the project manager must be able to delegate effectively and empower their team members to take ownership of their work.

The combination of technical knowledge and leadership skills allows the project manager to be successful in their role. With a strong technical background, they are able to make informed decisions and provide guidance and support to the development team. With strong leadership skills, they are able to motivate and engage their team and create a positive work environment that fosters collaboration and team-work.

In this example, the connection between leadership and technical expertise is clear. Without a strong technical background, the project manager would not be able to effectively lead the development team. Without strong leadership skills, the project manager would not be able to create a positive work environment, delegate effectively, or motivate and engage the team. Ultimately, the combination of these two skills allows the project manager to be a successful leader and to achieve great success in their career.

PART-9

AGILE
LEADERSHIP

Agile leadership is a leadership style that prioritises adaptability, collaboration, and continuous improvement. It is based on the principles of Agile methodology, which is a set of values and practices that originated from the software development industry. Agile methodology has since been adopted by organisations in a variety of industries, including healthcare, finance, and government.

Agile leaders value collaboration, communication, and transparency, and they prioritise the delivery of value to customers. They believe that teams should be self-organizing and cross-functional, and they empower team members to make decisions and take ownership of their work. Agile leaders also believe in continuous learning and improvement, and they seek to create a culture of experimentation and innovation.

One of the key features of Agile leadership is adaptability. Agile leaders are comfortable with ambiguity and uncertainty, and they are able to respond quickly to changing conditions and new information. They understand that the needs and expectations of customers can change quickly, and they are able to adjust their plans and strategies accordingly.

Another key aspect of Agile leadership is the focus on continuous improvement. Agile leaders believe that organisations and individuals can always be better, and they seek to create an environment that supports continuous learning and improvement. They encourage team members to experiment and try new things, and they are open to feedback and constructive criticism.

Agile leaders also prioritise communication and collaboration. They believe that teams are stronger when they work together, and they seek to create a positive and supportive work environment. They encourage open and honest communication and work to build trust and maintain positive relationships with team members.

Agile leaders are also focused on creating a sense of purpose and meaning for their teams. They believe that work should be more than just a job, and they seek to create a sense of purpose and meaning for their team members. They encourage team members to think about how their work contributes to the larger organisation and to society and help team members see the impact that they are making.

Agile leadership can be applied in a variety of settings, including businesses, government organisations, and non-profit organisations. It is particularly well-suited for organisations that operate in rapidly changing and complex environments and those that prioritise customer satisfaction and continuous improvement.

In order to be an effective Agile leader, it is important to have a deeper understanding of Agile methodology and the principles that underlie it. This includes understanding the values and practices of Agile methodology, such as collaboration, transparency, and continuous improvement and having the ability to apply these principles in a practical and effective manner.

Agile leaders must also be able to lead and influence their teams effectively. This requires a combination of technical and interpersonal skills, including the ability to motivate and inspire team members, manage team performance and progress, and build trust and maintain positive relationships with team members.

Agile leaders must also be able to think critically and creatively and make effective decisions in complex and dynamic environments. They must be able to understand the needs and expectations of customers and balance the needs of different stakeholders in a rapidly changing environment.

Agile leadership is based on the principles of Agile methodology, and it is well-suited for organisations that operate in rapidly changing and complex environments. Effective Agile leaders have a deeper understanding of Agile methodology and the principles that underlie it, and they have the technical and interpersonal skills necessary to lead and influence teams effectively.

Agility in leadership refers to the ability of a leader to adapt quickly and effectively to changing circumstances, situations, and environments. The ability to be agile is becoming increasingly important in today's fast-paced, rapidly changing world, where businesses and organisations are facing new challenges and opportunities every day. Leaders who are agile are better equipped to navigate through uncertainty and risk and lead their teams and organisations to success.

One of the key components of agility in leadership is the ability to be flexible and open-minded. Agile leaders are able to pivot their strategies and approaches as new information and circumstances arise rather than sticking rigidly to a set plan. They are able to see the bigger picture and understand the interconnections between different aspects of a situation, which enables them to make informed decisions that take into account the long-term consequences of their actions.

Another important aspect of agility in leadership is the ability to quickly identify and respond to new opportunities. Agile leaders are able to spot new trends and changes in the marketplace or in the business environment and are able to respond quickly and effectively to these changes. They are not afraid to try new things and take calculated risks, and they understand that failure is an inevitable part of the innovation process.

Agile leaders also understand the importance of teamwork and collaboration. They are able to create an environment where their team members feel comfortable sharing ideas and taking calculated risks and where everyone is encouraged to contribute and take ownership of their work. This fosters a culture of innovation and creativity, where everyone is working together to achieve a common goal.

One of the benefits of agility in leadership is that it helps leaders to stay ahead of the curve. By being able to quickly identify and respond to changes in the business environment, agile leaders are able to stay ahead of the competition and position their organisations for long-term success.

Another benefit is that agility in leadership enables organisations to be more efficient and effective. Agile leaders are able
to make decisions quickly, which allows their organisations
to respond faster to new opportunities and challenges. This
can lead to improved productivity, increased profitability,
and a more engaged and motivated workforce.

There are several key attributes that define an agile leader.
Firstly, they are comfortable with ambiguity and uncertainty, and they can make decisions in the absence of complete
information. Secondly, they are adept at learning and continuously improving on it, and they embrace change as an
opportunity to grow. Thirdly, they are flexible and adaptable,
and they are able to pivot quickly when necessary.

The impact of agile leadership can be significant. Research
shows that organisations with agile leaders are more likely
to outperform their competitors and achieve their strategic
goals. A study by McKinsey & Company found that organisations with agile leaders had 12% higher shareholder returns
compared to those without agile leaders.

Another study by the Harvard Business Review found that
companies with agile leaders were 70% more likely to have
successful digital transformations. This is because agile
leaders are better able to recognise and respond to changing
customer needs and leverage technology to create new value
for their customers.

In terms of specific financial impacts, agile leaders are able
to reduce costs by streamlining processes and eliminating
waste, and they are better able to capitalise on new business
opportunities. For example, an agile leader may be able to

quickly identify and respond to a new market trend, leading to the launch of a new product or service that generates significant revenue growth.

Developing agility in leadership is essential in today's fast-paced, rapidly changing business environment. Being agile means being able to adapt quickly to new situations, change direction when necessary, and make quick decisions that impact the organisation positively.

Here are the steps to develop agility in leadership:

Embrace change: Leaders who are agile embrace change, view it as an opportunity for growth and innovation and are not afraid to take calculated risks.

Encourage collaboration: Agile leaders foster an environment of collaboration and teamwork, where diverse perspectives and experiences are valued, and everyone is encouraged to contribute.

Stay informed: Stay informed about the latest trends, technologies, and best practices in the industry. Regularly seek out new information and continue to learn and grow as a leader.

Empower your team: Give your team the autonomy to make decisions and act on their own while still providing guidance and support when needed.

Practice open communication: Encourage open communication between all members of the organisation, and be transparent and honest in your own communication.

Foster a culture of continuous improvement: Create a culture where everyone is encouraged to continuously learn, grow and improve.

Encourage experimentation: Encourage your team to experiment and try new approaches to problems and situations. This helps the team to be more agile and innovative.

Lead by example: Model the behaviour you want to see in your team, such as embracing change, being open to new ideas, and being flexible.

Reward success: Celebrate and reward success when it is achieved, and also reward the process of experimentation and continuous improvement.

Celebrate failure: Encourage your team to take risks and embrace failure as an opportunity to learn and grow.

By following these steps, leaders can develop the agility needed to succeed in today's dynamic business environment. However, developing agility is a continuous process that requires effort and a commitment to growth and improvement. It is, therefore, important for leaders to consistently implement these practices in order to become more agile over time.

Agility in leadership is becoming increasingly important in today's fast-paced, rapidly changing world. Leaders who are able to adapt quickly and effectively to new situations and circumstances are better equipped to lead their organisations to success. To develop agility in leadership, leaders need to be flexible and open-minded, be able to quickly identify and respond to new opportunities, understand the importance of teamwork and collaboration, and be willing to take calculated risks. By developing their agility, leaders can stay ahead of the curve, be more efficient and effective, and position their organisations for long-term success.

PART-10

LEADERSHIP
LIMITATIONS

Leadership is a critical component of organisational success and an essential factor in creating a high-performing team and a successful business. Despite the importance of leadership, there are several limitations that leaders must be aware of and navigate through in order to be effective. Understanding these limitations is crucial for leaders who want to achieve their goals and lead their organisations to success.

One of the main limitations of leadership is the personal limitations of the leader. Leaders are human and have their own biases, weaknesses, and limitations in their decision-making ability. For example, a leader may have a personal bias that prevents him/her from making decisions objectively or from considering all perspectives. This can lead to poor decision-making and can impact the effectiveness of their leadership. Leaders must be aware of their personal limitations and work to overcome them in order to make better and more informed decisions that benefit the organisation.

Another limitation of leadership is time constraints. Leaders have limited time to perform all their duties and may not be able to fully address all issues facing their organisation. This can lead to priorities being neglected, important initiatives being put on hold, and important decisions being delayed.

Leaders must be strategic in their time management and ensure that they are allocating their time effectively to address the most pressing issues facing the organisation.

Limited resources are another significant limitation of leadership. Leaders may have limited money and manpower to address challenges and implement their vision. This can make it difficult to achieve their goals and can limit their ability to drive change in the organisation. Leaders must be resourceful in finding ways to maximise the resources available to them and must be strategic in their allocation of resources to ensure that their goals are achieved.

Resistance to change is another limitation of leadership. Some followers may resist change and resist the leader's efforts to implement new ideas or policies. This can be due to a variety of reasons, such as a lack of understanding of the change, a lack of buy-in, or a fear of the unknown. Leaders must be skilled in managing resistance to change and must work to build support for their initiatives by effectively communicating their vision and addressing the concerns of their followers.

Lack of transparency is another limitation of leadership. Leaders may lack transparency in their decision-making process, which can erode trust and credibility with their followers. This can lead to feelings of mistrust and disengagement among followers and can make it difficult for the leader to achieve their goals. Leaders must be transparent in their decision-making and must communicate effectively with their followers to build trust and credibility.

Power imbalances are another limitation of leadership. Leaders may have unequal power and authority, which can create imbalances and lead to unethical behaviour. For example, a leader with too much power may abuse their authority and make decisions that are not in the best interest of the organisation or its followers. Leaders must be mindful of power imbalances and must work to maintain a balance of power in order to ensure ethical behaviour and maintain the trust and credibility of their followers.

Organisational politics is another limitation of leadership. Organisational politics can limit a leader's effectiveness by creating internal conflicts and hindering their ability to achieve their goals. Political manoeuvring, power struggles, and hidden agendas can undermine a leader's efforts to create a positive organisational culture and achieve their goals. Leaders must be skilled in navigating through organisational politics and must work to build a positive organisational culture that promotes collaboration and teamwork.

Limited scope of influence is another limitation of leadership. A leader's scope of influence may be limited to their immediate environment, and they may not have the ability to effect change on a larger scale. For example, a leader within a small department may have limited ability to impact change at the organisational level. Leaders must be aware of their scope of influence and must work to maximise their impact by building relationships and collaborating.

PART-11

LEADERSHIP
FIELDS AND
OPTIONS

L eadership paths and options can vary greatly depending on an individual's goals, experience, skills, and interests. However, some common paths and options include:

Entrepreneurial Leadership: This path involves starting and running one's own business. Entrepreneurial leaders are responsible for every aspect of the business, from developing the product or service to sales, marketing, and finances. These leaders must possess a unique combination of vision, creativity, and business acumen to successfully build and run their businesses. Entrepreneurial leaders must be able to identify and seize new opportunities, take risks, and make tough decisions in the face of uncertainty.

Corporate Leadership: This path involves working within a large or mid-sized company in a management or executive role. Corporate leaders are responsible for managing teams, setting strategies, and making decisions that impact the company as a whole. These leaders must be able to work effectively with stakeholders across the organisation, build a consensus around decisions, and motivate and inspire their teams to achieve their goals. Corporate leaders must also be well-versed in finance, operations, and business strategies to make informed decisions that drive growth and profitability.

Non-Profit Leadership: This path involves working in a leadership role within a non-profit organisation. Non-profit leaders are responsible for developing and implementing programs and initiatives that align with the organisation's mission and values. These leaders must be able to balance the needs of the organisation with the needs of the communities they serve and make decisions that reflect the organisation's core values. Non-profit leaders must also be able to build and manage partnerships, secure funding, and communicate effectively to mobilise support for their initiatives.

Political Leadership: This path involves working in a political role, such as a politician, lobbyist, or activist. Political leaders are responsible for advocating for policies and initiatives that align with their beliefs and values. These leaders must be able to articulate their vision and ideas effectively and build coalitions to support their initiatives. Political leaders must also be able to navigate through complex political landscapes and make decisions that reflect the needs and interests of their constituents.

Community Leadership: This path involves taking on a leadership role within a community, such as a neighbourhood, school district, or social group. Community leaders are responsible for improving the lives of those within their community and addressing community-wide issues. These leaders must be able to build relationships and mobilise support for their initiatives and make decisions that reflect the values and needs of the community. Community leaders must also be able to work effectively with stakeholders from different backgrounds and perspectives.

Military Leadership: This path involves serving in a leadership role within the military. Military leaders are responsible for leading and managing troops and making decisions that impact the safety and security of their country. These leaders must be able to make quick, informed decisions in high-pressure situations and inspire and motivate their troops to achieve their goals. Military leaders must also be able to effectively manage resources and build strong relationships with other military leaders and government officials.

It's important to note that these paths are not mutually exclusive, and individuals may choose to pursue multiple paths throughout their careers. Additionally, leadership development can occur within any role, regardless of the specific path or industry, through on-the-job experience, mentorship, and professional development opportunities. For example, an entrepreneur may choose to obtain additional education or training in finance or marketing to enhance their leadership skills, or a corporate leader may choose to serve as a mentor or coach to develop their leadership abilities in a new context. Ultimately, the path and options for leadership will depend on an individual's unique goals, skills, and interests, as well as the opportunities available to them. It's, therefore, important for leaders to reflect continuously.

PART-12

LEADERSHIP SCIENCE, METHODOLOGY, AND SKILLS

L eadership is a complex and multi-dimensional concept that involves several different aspects. While it may be challenging to pin down exactly what leadership is, there is a growing consensus that it involves a combination of science, methodology, skills, and characteristics.

From a scientific perspective, leadership has been studied and researched in various fields, such as psychology, sociology, and organisational behaviour. This has led to the development of various theories and models that help us to understand the dynamics and processes of leadership. For example, trait theory posits that leaders have certain innate traits that set them apart from others, while the situational leadership theory suggests that the most effective leadership style depends on the situation. Contingency theories emphasise that leaders must adapt their style to fit the situation, while the transformational leadership theory emphasises the importance of inspiring and motivating followers towards a shared vision.

In addition to scientific theories, leadership also involves the use of methodologies. This includes using specific techniques and approaches to achieve desired results. For example, leaders may use agile methodologies to manage complex projects or use decision-making frameworks to make strategic decisions. Effective leaders are able to understand the different methodologies available to them and choose the one that best suits their needs and the needs of their followers.

Skills are also a critical component of effective leadership. Effective leaders possess a set of specific skills, such as communication, problem-solving, and decision-making. Communication skills are essential for leaders to clearly and effectively convey their vision and ideas to followers, while problem-solving skills allow leaders to find creative solutions to complex challenges. Decision-making skills are also important for leaders to be able to make tough choices in a timely and effective manner.

Finally, leadership involves certain characteristics, such as integrity, vision, and emotional intelligence. Integrity refers to the ability of leaders to act with honesty and ethics, even in challenging circumstances. A strong vision is essential for leaders to inspire and motivate followers toward a common goal, while emotional intelligence allows leaders to understand the emotions of their followers and use this insight to connect and build trust with them.

Effective leaders are able to use their understanding of these different elements of leadership to guide and inspire their followers toward a shared vision. It is important to note that while some people may possess certain innate traits that make them naturally effective leaders, leadership is also a skill that can be developed and improved over time through education, experience, and self-reflection.

EXAMPLE:

An example of a leader who embodies the combination of science, methodology, skills, and characteristics is Steve Jobs. Jobs was well known for his innovative vision and charismatic personality, but he also relied on a systematic and data-driven approach to leadership.

From a scientific perspective, Jobs understood the importance of market research and customer insights in driving product development and innovation. He was known for his ability to anticipate trends and customer needs and also known for his willingness to pivot and change direction based on the data.

From a methodological perspective, Jobs was a stickler for efficiency and process and was known for his relentless pursuit of excellence. He established clear goals and expectations for his team and held himself and others accountable for delivering high-quality products and services.

From a skills perspective, Jobs was a master communicator and motivator who was able to inspire and engage his team and rally them around a common vision. He was also an expert problem-solver and decision-maker who was able to make tough calls and navigate through complex challenges.

From a characteristic perspective, Jobs was a natural leader who was known for his creativity, passion, and intensity. He was a visionary who was able to articulate a clear and compelling vision for his organisation and also inspire others to follow him.

In conclusion, Steve Jobs was a leader who combined a scientific, methodological, skills-based, and character-driven approach to leadership and was able to lead his organisation to remarkable success. By embracing these different perspectives and approaches, leaders can increase their effectiveness, impact, and legacy and make a lasting impact on the world.

PART-13

RELATIONSHIPS AND LEADERSHIP

Leadership and relationships are intricately linked, as effective leadership requires a deeper understanding of the people and groups being led, the ability to build trust and rapport with them, and the ability to engage and motivate them to achieve shared goals. A leader who is skilled at building relationships can create a positive and supportive work environment, foster collaboration, and build a culture of trust and respect.

One of the key ways in which leaders can build relationships is by engaging with their employees, customers, partners, and other stakeholders in open and honest communication. This requires leaders to listen actively, to be transparent and authentic in their interactions, and to be responsive to the needs and concerns of others. When leaders engage in active listening, they are better able to understand the perspectives of others, address their concerns, and build trust and rapport.

Another way in which leaders can build relationships is by creating a culture of transparency, inclusiveness, and collaboration. This requires leaders to be open and honest about their intentions, goals, and expectations and be willing to engage in constructive dialogue with others. When leaders foster a culture of transparency, inclusiveness, and collaboration, they are better able to create a work environment that is supportive, empowering, and inclusive and build a sense of community among employees.

Leadership also requires the ability to build strong relationships with customers, as this is essential for providing high-quality products and services and fostering customer loyalty. Leaders who are able to build strong relationships with their customers are better able to understand their needs, provide personalised and effective solutions, and foster customer loyalty. When customers feel valued and respected by their leaders, they are more likely to remain loyal, provide positive feedback, and recommend the organisation to others.

Finally, leaders who are able to build strong relationships with partners and other members of the community are better able to foster collaboration, achieve common goals, and build a positive reputation for their organisation. When leaders are able to build trust and respect with other stakeholders, they are better able to build partnerships and achieve shared success.

Leaders who are skilled at building relationships are better able to be successful, build trust and respect, and make a lasting impact on their organisations and communities. Effective leadership requires the ability to engage in open and honest communication to create a culture of transparency, inclusiveness, and collaboration that builds strong relationships with customers and fosters partnerships and collaboration with other stakeholders. By investing in relationship-building, leaders can create a supportive, empowering, and inclusive work environment and build a culture of trust and respect.

PART-14

NATURAL LEADERSHIP, EARNED AND ACQUIRED

There is an ongoing debate about whether leadership is an innate quality or something that can be acquired through education, training, and practical experience. In reality, the answer lies somewhere between ideologies.

On one hand, there are certain personality traits that can be beneficial for leadership. For example, charismatic individuals who are confident and assertive may have an easier time inspiring and motivating others. In addition, certain cognitive abilities, such as emotional intelligence and the ability to think creatively and outside the box, can also be advantageous for leaders.

However, simply possessing these traits is not enough to guarantee success as a leader. There are numerous other skills and competencies that are essential for effective leadership, including strategic thinking, decision-making, problem-solving, communication, and interpersonal skills. These skills can be developed and refined through education, training, and practical experience.

Moreover, the most effective leaders are not only technically competent but also have the ability to connect with and inspire their team members. They have strong interpersonal skills, are able to build and maintain positive relationships, and create a sense of community and teamwork among their followers. This requires a deeper understanding of human behaviour and the ability to navigate through complex social dynamics.

Therefore, it can be said that leadership is both innately given and earned or acquired. While some individuals may have a natural talent for leadership, effective leadership also requires ongoing learning and development, as well as practical experiences in applying the skills and knowledge acquired through education and training.

Additionally, it is worth noting that even individuals who possess natural leadership traits may struggle to lead effectively if they lack the necessary skills and competencies. Conversely, individuals who have developed their leadership skills through education and training may be highly effective leaders, even if they do not possess natural leadership traits.

Leadership is a complex phenomenon that is influenced by a range of factors, including both nature and nurture. While some researchers argue that certain personality traits, such as extroversion, emotional intelligence, and cognitive abilities, may be partially determined by genetics, it is widely accepted that leadership is not solely a result of one's DNA.

On one hand, some individuals may be naturally predisposed to certain leadership traits, such as charisma, confidence, and assertiveness. These individuals may have an easier time inspiring and motivating others, communicating their vision, and building strong relationships with their followers. However, simply having these traits is not enough to be an effective leader.

On the other hand, leadership skills and abilities can also be developed and acquired through experiences, education, and training. For example, a leader can learn how to communicate effectively, make strategic decisions, delegate responsibilities, and build teams through a combination of formal education, on-the-job training, and self-study. Moreover, the continuous exposure to different leadership styles and the opportunity to reflect on their own experiences and learn from their mistakes can help individuals develop their leadership skills and abilities over time.

While genetics may play a role in shaping certain personality traits that are relevant to leadership, leadership is not solely determined by one's DNA. Rather, leadership is a combination of inherent traits, life experiences, and learned skills that come together to shape an individual's leadership style and effectiveness. Effective leaders are those who have developed a unique blend of innate traits and acquired skills that allow them to effectively lead, motivate, and inspire their teams.

PART-15

LEADERSHIP IN CHILDREN

Developing leadership skills and personalities in children is a crucial task for parents, teachers, and caregivers. Leadership skills are essential for success in various areas of life, including personal, academic, and professional lives. Children who learn to become effective leaders at an early age will become well-equipped to handle life's challenges and be more successful in both their personal and professional lives. Here are some ways to develop leadership skills in children:

Encourage them to take the initiative: Encourage your child to take the initiative and be responsible. Give them opportunities to make decisions, solve problems, and take on projects. Encourage them to be proactive, and help them understand the importance of taking ownership of their own actions.

Teach them to be responsible: Teach your child to be responsible and accountable for their actions. Encourage them to keep their promises and commitments, and help them understand the consequences of not following through. This will help build their sense of responsibility and further help them develop leadership skills.

Foster teamwork: Teamwork is an essential component of leadership. Encourage your child to work with others and learn to collaborate. Teach them to appreciate the different perspectives and strengths of others and work together to achieve a common goal.

Encourage them to be confident: Confidence is a critical component of leadership. Encourage your child to be confident, speak up, and share their thoughts and ideas. Encourage them to take risks and try new things, and help them understand that failure is a natural part of the learning process.

Develop their communication skills: Good communication skills are essential for leadership. Encourage your child to communicate effectively and to listen actively. Teach them to articulate their thoughts and ideas clearly and concisely and communicate their ideas in a respectful and professional manner.

Teach them to be adaptable: Adaptability is a key component of leadership. Encourage your child to be flexible and open-minded, and be willing to change their approach when necessary. Teach them to be adaptable, and embrace change and new challenges.

Encourage them to be resilient: Resilience is a critical component of leadership. Encourage your child to be resilient, and bounce back from setbacks and challenges. Teach them to be persistent and never give up, and help them understand that success often requires perseverance.

Develop their emotional intelligence: Emotional intelligence is a critical component of leadership. Encourage your child to understand and manage their emotions and also empathise with others. Teach them to be aware of their own emotions, and understand how their emotions affect others.

Teach them to set and achieve goals: Encourage your child to set goals and work towards achieving them. Teach them to be goal-oriented, and understand the importance of setting and achieving goals.

Provide opportunities for leadership: Provide your child with opportunities to practice their leadership skills. Encourage them to take on leadership roles, whether it be in school, sports, or other activities. Provide opportunities for your child to lead and cause them to learn from their experiences.

By fostering the development of key leadership skills, such as initiative, responsibility, teamwork, confidence, communication, adaptability, resilience, emotional intelligence, goal-setting, and providing leadership opportunities, you can help your child grow into a confident, competent, and effective leader.

> *"Give me a child until he is 7 and I will show you the man."*
> *- Philosopher and educator Aristotle.*

The quote by Aristotle has been widely quoted and discussed in many fields, including education, psychology, philosophy, and leadership studies. The idea behind this quote is that a person's basic personality traits, habits, and tendencies are largely established in their early childhood days and are shaped by their environment, family, education, and experiences. For example, a child who is exposed to positive role models and experiences, such as nurturing parents, good teachers, and supportive friends, is more likely to develop healthy self-esteem, confidence, and empathy, which are all qualities that are important for effective leadership.

In contrast, a child who is exposed to negative experiences, such as abuse, neglect, or bullying, is more likely to develop low self-esteem, negative attitudes, and behavioural problems, which can negatively impact their leadership potential and performance. Therefore, it is important to provide children with positive experiences and support that help them develop into confident, resilient, and empathetic adults who are capable of effective leadership.

However, it is also important to note that this quote does not mean that a person's character and leadership potential are fully formed and unchanging by the age of seven. While early childhood experiences can have a lasting impact on a person's personality and leadership style, it is also possible for individuals to change, grow, and develop as leaders throughout their lives. This can be achieved through education, training, coaching, mentoring, and exposure to new experiences and challenges.

Leadership development is a lifelong journey that requires continuous learning and growth. A good leader must be willing to reflect on their strengths and weaknesses and seek out opportunities to improve their leadership skills and knowledge. They must also be flexible and adaptable and be willing to learn from their experiences and challenges.

For example, a leader who is strong in technical skills but weak in interpersonal skills can take courses in communication and conflict resolution, seek feedback from their team members, and practice active listening and empathy to improve their relationship-building skills. Again, a leader who is prone to procrastination can work on developing better time-management strategies and habits, such as setting clear goals, prioritizing tasks, and delegating responsibilities.

While a person's leadership potential may be influenced by their early childhood experiences and personality traits, it is not predetermined or set in stone. Effective leadership can be learned, developed, and refined throughout a person's lifetime through education, training, experience, and self-reflection. A good leader is constantly seeking opportunities to improve their skills, knowledge, and abilities and is also willing to invest time and effort into their personal and professional growth.

PART-16

DEVELOPING EMOTIONAL INTELLIGENCE

Emotional intelligence (EI) is the ability to understand and manage emotions, both personally and those of others. EI is a critical component of effective leadership, as it enables leaders to navigate through complex social and interpersonal situations, build strong relationships, and foster positive team dynamics. In this section, we will explore the key components of EI and the strategies that leaders can use to develop their emotional intelligence.

SELF-AWARENESS

The first component of EI is self-awareness, which refers to the ability to understand and recognise one's own emotions, values, and strengths. Self-aware leaders have a clearer understanding of what makes them feel frustrated, angry, or happy, and they are able to use this knowledge to regulate their emotions and make informed decisions. One effective way to develop self-awareness is to engage in regular self-reflection and introspection and examine one's thoughts, feelings, and motivations. Leaders can also use journaling, coaching, or therapy to gain a deeper understanding of their emotional landscape.

EMOTIONAL REGULATION

The second component of EI is emotional regulation, which refers to the ability to manage one's own emotions effectively. Leaders with high emotional regulation are able to stay calm and centred even in challenging situations, allowing them to make clear and rational decisions. To develop emotional regulation, leaders can use various stress management techniques such as deep breathing, mindfulness, or exercise. Additionally, leaders can work to identify their triggers and learn strategies for managing their emotions in those situations.

EMPATHY

Empathetic leaders are able to connect with their team members, build strong relationships, and foster a supportive work environment. To develop empathy, leaders can engage in active listening, practice putting themselves in others' shoes, and seek feedback from others to gain a deeper understanding of their perspective.

SOCIAL SKILLS

The final component of EI is social skills, which refer to the ability to effectively navigate through social and interpersonal situations. Leaders with strong social skills are able to build trust and rapport with others, manage conflicts, and effectively communicate their vision and goals. To develop social skills, leaders can participate in interpersonal skills training, seek feedback from others, and engage in role-playing exercises to build their confidence and effectiveness in social situations.

There are many strategies that leaders can use to develop their emotional intelligence. Whether through self-reflection and introspection, stress management techniques, empathy exercises, or interpersonal skills training, leaders can build their emotional intelligence and become more effective and influential in their leadership roles. By cultivating a deeper understanding of their own emotions and those of others around them, leaders can create a supportive work environment, build strong relationships, and foster positive team dynamics, leading to improved organisational outcomes and long-term success.

PART-17

DEVELOPING
TRUST

One of the most critical elements of effective leadership is trust. Without trust, leaders will struggle to build strong relationships with their followers, and the success of their efforts will be limited. In this section, we will explore the importance of trust in leadership and discuss practical steps that leaders can take to build trust with their followers.

Trust is an essential component of effective leadership because it forms the foundation of all relationships. When people trust their leaders, they are more likely to be engaged, motivated, and committed to their work. Trust also promotes open and honest communication, which is essential for making informed decisions and solving problems effectively. Trusted leaders are also more likely to receive support from their followers during times of change and uncertainty.

Building trust as a leader requires a combination of personal characteristics and behaviours. Leaders must be transparent, honest, and ethical in their dealings with others. They must also be reliable and consistent in their actions, which builds credibility and demonstrates their commitment to their followers. Leaders who are approachable and genuine in their interactions with others are also more likely to build trust.

One of the most effective ways to build trust as a leader is through open and honest communication. Leaders should be transparent about their goals, strategies, and decision-making processes. They should also involve their followers in the decision-making process and be open to feedback and input. This shows that leaders value the perspectives of others and are committed to building relationships based on mutual respect and understanding.

Another important aspect of building trust as a leader is being accountable for one's actions. Leaders must take responsibility for their decisions and be willing to admit mistakes when they occur. This demonstrates integrity and a commitment to transparency, which are critical elements of trust. Leaders should also be consistent in their behaviour and follow through on commitments, which builds credibility and demonstrates their reliability.

Leaders can also build trust by being supportive and empathetic toward their followers. This means being understanding and compassionate when others face challenges and being willing to lend a helping hand when needed. Leaders who are supportive and empathetic create a positive work environment and foster stronger relationships with their followers.

Finally, leaders must be able to build trust through their actions. This means consistently demonstrating the values and principles that are important to the organisation and its stakeholders. Leaders should also be role models, embodying the behaviours and attitudes they wish to see in their followers.

Trust is a critical component of effective leadership. Leaders who are able to build trust with their followers are more likely to be successful in their efforts to achieve organisational goals. Building trust requires a combination of personal characteristics and behaviours, including open and honest communication, accountability, supportiveness, and being a role model. By focusing on these key elements, leaders can build stronger relationships with their followers and create a positive and productive work environment.

PART-18

NEURO-LINGUISTIC PROGRAMMING (NLP) IN LEADERSHIP

Neuro-Linguistic Programming (NLP) is a field of study that combines the principles of psychology, linguistics, and communication. It was developed in the 1970s by Richard Bandler and John Grinder, who were interested in exploring how people communicate and how they can be more effective in their communication. NLP is based on the idea that language and behaviour are interconnected and that by understanding the relationship between language and behaviour, we can improve our communication skills, change our behaviours, and achieve our goals more effectively.

A leader must be able to motivate, inspire, and guide a team of people toward a common goal. A leader must also be able to communicate effectively, resolve conflicts, make decisions, and manage stress.

The relationship between NLP and leadership is that NLP can help leaders develop the skills and attitudes needed to be effective. NLP provides leaders with a set of tools and techniques for improving their communication skills, managing their emotions, and achieving their goals. By using NLP, leaders can gain greater insights into their own thoughts, behaviours, and motivations. They can also learn how to use language more effectively to influence others.

One of the key techniques in NLP is rapport building. Rapport building involves establishing a connection with others by using similar language patterns, body language, and gestures. Leaders who are skilled at rapport building are better able to communicate with their team members and establish a sense of trust and collaboration.

Another important aspect of NLP is the use of reframing. Reframing involves changing the way we think about a situation by changing our focus and perspective. Leaders who are skilled at reframing are better able to manage stress, resolve conflicts, and find creative solutions to problems.

NLP also involves the use of anchoring, which is the process of creating an emotional or behavioural response to a specific stimulus. Leaders who are skilled at anchoring can use this technique to trigger positive emotions and behaviours in themselves and others. For example, a leader might anchor a positive memory or feeling of success to a particular gesture or phrase and then use that gesture or phrase to trigger positive emotions and behaviours whenever they need to motivate their team.

Finally, NLP involves the use of metaprogramming, which is the study of how we think and process information. Leaders who are skilled at metaprogramming can understand the thinking patterns and motivations of their team members and use this information to communicate more effectively and resolve conflicts.

The relationship between NLP and leadership is that NLP can help leaders develop the skills and attitudes needed to be effective leaders. By using NLP, leaders can improve their communication skills, manage their emotions, and achieve their goals. NLP provides leaders with a set of tools and techniques for building rapport, reframing situations, anchoring positive emotions and behaviours, and understanding the thinking patterns and motivations of their team members.

PART-19

LEADERSHIP CAUSE AND EFFECT

Leadership has been the subject of much debate and study over the years. While some argue that leadership is a cause that drives success and change, others believe that it is an effect that arises from other factors such as circumstance, experience, and personality. In this section, we will examine the latter perspective, exploring the ways in which leadership can be seen as an effect rather than a cause.

One of the key arguments for considering leadership as an effect is that it is often a result of situational factors. The environment and circumstances in which a person finds himself/herself can greatly impact their ability to lead and their effectiveness as a leader. For example, a person who is in a position of authority may have a different level of influence and impact than someone who is not. Similarly, a person who is faced with challenging circumstances, such as a crisis, may be more likely to take on a leadership role and exhibit strong leadership qualities. These situational factors can shape the way that a person behaves, influencing their actions and responses in a way that leads to effective leadership.

Another factor that contributes to leadership as an effect is experience. People who have faced challenging situations, or have been in leadership positions before, may be more equipped to lead and exhibit strong leadership skills again.

These experiences shape the way that a person thinks, acts, and communicates, allowing them to navigate through difficult circumstances and make decisions that have a positive impact on those around them. Experience also provides opportunities for personal growth, helping individuals to develop their emotional intelligence, communication skills, and resilience are so important for successful leadership.

Finally, personality is another factor that can impact the development of leadership skills and abilities. Some individuals are naturally more assertive, confident, and driven than others, which can make them more likely to take on leadership roles and be successful in these positions. However, it is important to note that while personality traits can play a role in shaping leadership abilities, they are not the only factor. A person with a naturally outgoing and confident personality may not have the skills and experience necessary to be an effective leader, while someone with a more introverted personality may develop stronger leadership skills through experience and training.

While leadership is often considered a cause of success and change, it is clear that it can also be seen as an effect that arises from a variety of factors, including situational factors, experience, and personality. Understanding these factors is essential for developing effective leadership skills and ensuring that leaders are able to navigate through challenging situations and drive positive change in their organisations and communities. By focusing on these factors and working to develop the skills and abilities that are so important for successful leadership, individuals can become effective leaders and help to drive positive change in the world.

While it is commonly thought of as a cause, in reality, leadership can also be seen as a collective description of outcomes. The focus on leadership as an outcome rather than a cause can provide a more comprehensive and nuanced understanding of this concept and how it impacts organisations and individuals.

Leadership is not simply the result of an individual's traits, characteristics, or behaviours. Instead, it is a complex interplay between the leader, followers, and the environment in which they interact. The actions and decisions of a leader impact the followers, and in turn, the followers' reactions and behaviours impact the leader. This creates a feedback loop that is dynamic and continually evolving.

In this sense, leadership can be considered an outcome because it is a result of the interactions between the leader and followers. The leader's effectiveness and impact are determined by the degree to which they are able to inspire, motivate, and guide their followers to achieve a common goal. Leaders who are able to create a positive work culture, foster collaboration and teamwork, and promote a sense of purpose and meaning, will be more effective in achieving their goals as leaders and will have a greater impact on their followers and organisation.

Leadership can also be considered an outcome because it is a reflection of the individual's impact on their followers and organisation. A leader's success and effectiveness are not simply a function of their personal characteristics and traits but also a function of the impact they have on others. For example, a leader who is able to create a positive and supportive work environment will not only inspire and motivate their followers but will also foster a culture of trust, collaboration, and innovation.

Leadership is also an outcome because it is a result of the individual's ability to adapt and respond to changes in the environment. Leaders who are able to effectively navigate through changes in their industry, organisation, or external environment will be better positioned to achieve their goals and have a greater impact on their followers and organisation.

Considering leadership as an outcome rather than a cause provides a more nuanced and comprehensive understanding of this complex concept. It recognises that leadership is a result of the interactions between the leader, followers, and the environment and that it is a reflection of the individual's impact on their followers and organisation. By focusing on leadership as an outcome, organisations and individuals can gain a deeper understanding of how to develop and foster effective leadership and create a more positive and impactful work culture.

PART-20

THE BALANCE OF LEADERSHIP

Leadership is an essential aspect of life that can shape an individual's personality, growth, and success. While many people believe that leadership is a fixed trait that one possesses, it is instead a combination of learned skills, natural qualities, and experiences. A leader who strives for balance in their life can be more effective, resilient, and inspiring to those around them. In this section, we will discuss the importance of balancing different aspects of life as a leader and offer tips on how to create a balance in leadership.

First and foremost, it is crucial for a leader to understand that there is no one-size-fits-all approach to balancing their life. Every leader is unique and will have different priorities, strengths, and weaknesses. However, there are some common areas that leaders can focus on to create a balance in their life.

Work-Life Balance: One of the most critical areas of life to balance is work and personal life. Leaders are often under a great deal of pressure to perform at work and may find themselves working longer hours or sacrificing their personal life to meet deadlines or achieve goals. It is important for leaders to understand that taking care of themselves and their personal life is just as important as work. Leaders who can create a balance between work and personal life are more likely to be productive, motivated, and happy in their careers.

Health and Well-being: Leaders who take care of their physical, mental, and emotional health are better equipped to lead people effectively. Taking care of one's health involves engaging in regular exercise, eating a balanced diet, getting enough sleep, and reducing stress. A healthy leader is more focused, creative, and energised and is better able to make informed decisions and manage challenges.

Personal Growth: Leaders who invest in their personal growth and development are better equipped to lead others. Personal growth can involve pursuing new hobbies, learning new skills, reading books, attending workshops, or any other activity that broadens one's knowledge and skills. A leader who invests in personal growth is more confident, adaptable, and innovative.

Relationships: Strong relationships are critical to a leader's success. Leaders who have a supportive network of friends, family, and colleagues are more likely to feel fulfilled and satisfied in their lives. It is, therefore, important for leaders to nurture their relationships and invest time and effort into building stronger and more positive connections.

Financial Stability: Leaders who are financially stable are better equipped to lead effectively. Financial stability involves creating a budget, saving money, and reducing debt. Leaders who are financially stable are less stressed and more focused on their work and personal life.

By balancing these different aspects of life, leaders can create a foundation for success and personal growth. However, achieving balance in life is not always easy and often requires intentional effort and discipline. Here are some tips for creating a balance in leadership and other aspects of life:

Prioritise: Leaders should identify their priorities and focus on the areas of their life that are most important to them. By prioritizing their life, leaders can ensure that they are putting their time and energy into the things that matter the most.

Set boundaries: Leaders should set clear boundaries between work and personal life to ensure that they are not sacrificing their personal life for work. This can involve setting specific work hours, limiting work-related activities during personal time, and delegating tasks to others.

Plan ahead: Leaders should plan ahead and schedule time for different activities, including work, personal life, and personal growth. This helps them to ensure that they are using their time effectively and not overextending themselves.

Seek support: Leaders should seek support from friends, family, and colleagues. Having a support system can help leaders manage their challenges and achieve their goals.

The importance of balancing different aspects of life, such as work-life balance, health and well-being, personal growth, relationships, and financial stability, for a more effective and resilient leader, was discussed. Leaders should prioritise their life, set boundaries, plan ahead, and seek a support system to create balance in their lives. By doing so, they can create a foundation for success and personal growth.

PART-21

LEADERSHIP IN SOCIAL AND MARITAL LIFE

Leadership skills are not only valuable in the workplace but also in personal life, especially in relationships such as social and marital life. Effective leadership can enhance communication, promote understanding, and bring happiness to both parties. In this section, we will explore how leadership can be applied to social and marital life and discuss the skills that are needed to be an effective leader in these relationships.

Communication: One of the most important skills for effective leadership in social and marriage life is good communication. Leaders need to be able to express their thoughts, feelings, and needs clearly and respectfully to others. This requires active listening, empathy, and the ability to understand the perspectives of others. Leaders should strive to create a safe and open environment where both parties feel heard and understood.

Empathy: Leaders who are empathetic are better equipped to understand the needs and emotions of others. Empathy involves considering someone's feelings and perspectives. By being empathetic, leaders can build trust and foster positive relationships in their social and marital lives.

Flexibility: Effective leaders are flexible and adaptable to changing circumstances. In social and marital life, this means being willing to compromise and finding creative solutions to problems. Leaders who are inflexible may struggle to maintain positive relationships and may cause conflicts.

Accountability: Leaders who take responsibility for their actions and decisions are more likely to be respected and trusted by others. In social and marital life, this means being accountable for one's behaviour and being willing to apologise and make amends when necessary. Leaders who take accountability for their actions demonstrate maturity and integrity.

Vision: Leaders who have a clear vision for their future are more likely to be successful in all aspects of life, including social and marital life. Having a vision provides direction and purpose and helps leaders stay focused and motivated. Leaders who share their vision with their partners can cause them to work together to create a future that they both desire.

Effective leadership in social and marital life requires a combination of communication, empathy, flexibility, accountability, and vision. By developing these skills, leaders can build stronger relationships, foster positive communication, and bring happiness to themselves and those around them. It is, therefore, important for leaders to continually work on their leadership skills, seeking feedback and seeking opportunities for growth and development.

PART-22

LEADERSHIP SACRIFICES AND HARDSHIPS

L eadership is an admirable and sought-after quality that is essential for success in many areas of life, including business, politics, and the community. However, it is important to understand that leadership comes with a certain set of sacrifices that must be made in order to be successful. In this section, we will explore the sacrifices that leaders must make in order to be effective and inspire change.

Time: One of the biggest sacrifices that leaders must make is to give their time. Leaders are often expected to work long hours, attend meetings, and engage with their constituents. This can be a challenge for those who have families, hobbies, and other commitments, but it is a necessary sacrifice if they want to be effective leaders. By prioritizing their work, leaders can ensure that they are using their time effectively and that they are making a positive impact in their communities.

Privacy: Another sacrifice that leaders must make is to give up their privacy. Leaders are often in the public eye and are expected to be transparent and accountable for their actions. This can be a challenge for those who value their privacy, but it is a necessary sacrifice if they want to be effective leaders. By being transparent and open, leaders can build trust with their constituents and demonstrate their commitment to their community.

Comforts: Leaders must also sacrifice their comfort and convenience in order to be effective. This can involve taking on difficult tasks, making tough decisions, and engaging with constituents who may have opposing views. Leaders who are willing to make these sacrifices are more likely to be respected and admired by their constituents and are better equipped to lead effectively.

Financial stability: Leaders must also be willing to sacrifice their finances in order to be effective. This can involve taking on leadership roles that may not be as lucrative as other positions or investing time and resources into their community. Leaders who are willing to make these sacrifices are more likely to be respected and admired by their constituents and are better equipped to lead effectively.

Personal life: Leaders must also be willing to sacrifice their personal life in order to be effective. This can involve working long hours, attending events outside of normal working hours, and putting the needs of their constituents above their own. Leaders who are willing to make these sacrifices are more likely to be respected and admired by their constituents and are better equipped to lead effectively.

Leadership is an essential aspect of human development, and it's crucial to identify the signs of leadership early on in life. Being able to identify the signs of leadership can help individuals cultivate and nurture these qualities, leading to a more fulfilling life and a better future. In this section, we will explore the signs of leadership and how they can be developed in children.

Communication skills: Effective communication is a vital aspect of leadership. Children who exhibit strong communication skills, such as being confident and articulate when speaking, are likely to be successful leaders. They can clearly express their thoughts and ideas and have the ability to listen to others. Encouraging children to participate in group discussions and presentations can help them to develop their communication skills.

Problem-solving skills: Effective leaders are able to find solutions to complex problems. Children who have a natural ability to find solutions to problems, even at a young age, are likely to have a bright future as leaders. Encouraging children to think critically and creatively when solving problems can help them develop this skill.

Empathy and compassion: Empathy and compassion are important traits of leaders. Children who have a strong sense of empathy and compassion are likely to be successful in their future careers. Encouraging children to help others and be kind to those around them can help them develop this trait.

Confidence: Confidence is a key characteristic of successful leaders. Children who exhibit confidence, even at a young age, are likely to be successful leaders in the future. Encouraging children to participate in new activities and experiences can help them build their confidence.

Resilience: Resilience is an essential trait for leaders, as they will often face challenges and obstacles in their careers. Children who exhibit resilience, even at a young age, are likely to be successful leaders in the future. Encouraging children to persevere and not give up when faced with obstacles can help them develop this trait.

Adaptability: Adaptability is a crucial trait for leaders, as they need to be able to adjust to new and changing circumstances. Children who exhibit adaptability, even at a young age, are likely to be successful leaders in the future. Encouraging children to try new things and be open-minded can help them develop this trait.

Positive Attitude: A positive attitude is a vital aspect of leadership. Children who exhibit a positive attitude, even at a young age, are likely to be successful leaders in the future. Encouraging children to see the good in others and have a positive outlook on life can help them develop this trait.

The signs of leadership can be identified early on in life and developed through various methods. Encouraging children to participate in new activities, to think critically and creatively, to have a positive attitude, and to be kind and compassionate to others can all help them to develop the essential traits of leadership. It is never too early to start developing leadership skills, and by identifying and nurturing these traits, children can have a successful and fulfilling future.

Leadership is a demanding and challenging role that requires a great deal of sacrifice. However, by making these sacrifices, leaders can inspire change, build trust, and make a positive impact in their communities. Whether you are leading a business, a political organisation, or a community group, it is important to understand the sacrifices that you will need to make in order to be effective. By being willing to make these sacrifices, you can build a legacy that will inspire others for years to come.

PART-23

LEADERSHIP REWARDS

Leadership is a demanding and challenging role that requires dedication, hard work, and commitment. While being a leader can come with its challenges, it also offers numerous rewards that can greatly enhance an individual's life. These rewards come in many forms and can have a profound impact on a leader's personal and professional growth. In this section, we will explore the many rewards of leadership and why they are worth the sacrifices and effort.

Personal Growth: One of the most significant rewards of leadership is personal growth. The leadership role requires individuals to take on new challenges, responsibilities, and tasks that push them out of their comfort zones and help them develop new skills and abilities. This process of personal growth and development can be incredibly fulfilling and empowering for leaders. As they continue to grow, leaders become more confident, self-assured, and resilient, which can have a positive impact on their personal and professional lives.

Influence: Leadership positions offer individuals the opportunity to influence and impact the lives of others. Leaders have the power to inspire, motivate, and guide others toward a common goal or vision. This influence can have a lasting impact on the lives of those they lead, making them feel valued and appreciated. For leaders, this sense of purpose and impact can be incredibly rewarding.

Recognition: Leaders who become successful in their roles often receive recognition and accolades from those they lead and from their peers. This recognition can be in the form of public praise, awards, or other forms of recognition. Receiving recognition for one's efforts and achievements is an excellent way to build up self-esteem and confidence and validate the sacrifices and hard work that went into achieving success.

Opportunities for Advancement: Leadership positions often come with opportunities for advancement. As leaders gain experience and demonstrate their skills, they may be offered new and more challenging roles within their organisations. These opportunities for advancement can lead to increased responsibility, higher salaries, and greater recognition from their peers.

Financial Rewards: Some leadership positions come with significant financial rewards, including higher salaries, bonuses, and other financial incentives. While these financial rewards of leadership should not be the primary motivator, they can provide leaders with a sense of financial security and stability. This financial stability can provide leaders with the freedom to focus on other aspects of their lives, including their personal and professional goals.

In conclusion, leadership comes with numerous rewards that can greatly enhance an individual's life. These rewards include personal growth, influence, recognition, opportunities for advancement, and financial rewards. While being a lead-

er requires dedication, hard work, and sacrifice, these rewards make the journey worth it. By embracing the rewards
of leadership, individuals can build fulfilling and meaningful
careers that have a positive impact on themselves and those
they lead.

PART-24

IMPLICATION OF NEGATIVE LEADERSHIP

Leadership plays a significant role in the success and prosperity of organisations, communities, and individuals. While positive leadership can bring great rewards, negative leadership can have serious financial implications. In this section, we will examine the financial consequences of negative leadership and how they can impact organisations and individuals.

Poor Decision Making: One of the biggest financial implications of negative leadership is poor decision making. Leaders who are ineffective, indecisive, or make decisions based on personal bias can cause financial losses for organisations and individuals. For example, leaders who make hasty decisions without proper research or analysis can result in investments that fail or cause significant financial losses.

Reduced Productivity: Negative leadership can also lead to reduced productivity. Leaders who are ineffective, disengaged, or lack a clear direction can create a lack of motivation and low morale among employees. This can result in decreased productivity as employees become demotivated and disengaged from their work.

Loss of Talented Employees: Negative leadership can lead to the loss of talented employees. Leaders who are ineffective, intimidating, or lack empathy can cause employees to feel undervalued, disrespected, or unsupported. This can result in high turnover rates, as employees leave in search of better working conditions or opportunities.

Decreased Revenue: Negative leadership can decrease revenue for organisations. Leaders who are ineffective, indecisive, or make poor decisions can cause financial losses, as well as damage to the organisation's reputation. A negative reputation can lead to decreased customer loyalty and reduced sales, which can result in decreased revenue.

Litigation Costs: Negative leadership can also increase litigation costs. Leaders who engage in unethical or illegal behaviour, or who discriminate against employees, can lead to lawsuits and legal fees. These legal fees can be significant, as organisations may need to defend themselves against lawsuits, as well as pay for damages to affected parties.

Negative leadership can have serious financial implications for organisations and individuals. Leaders who are ineffective, indecisive, or engage in unethical or illegal behaviour can result in decreased productivity, loss of talented employees, decreased revenue and increased litigation costs. It is, therefore, essential for organisations to invest in positive leadership and provide support and training to leaders to avoid the financial consequences of negative leadership.

Leadership plays a crucial role in determining the success of an organisation. It sets the tone for the company's culture, establishes its goals, and drives its direction. However, negative leadership can have serious consequences, including financial implications that can significantly impact the organisation. Negative leadership refers to leadership styles that are ineffective, harmful or lack ethical standards. This type of leadership can decrease employee morale, increase turnover, and decrease productivity, all of which can have a profound effect on an organisation's bottom line.

One of the primary financial implications of negative leadership is decreased productivity. Negative leaders often create a toxic work environment that demotivates employees and decreases their engagement levels. When employees are disengaged, they are less likely to be productive, and this can lead to decreased output and lower profits. Moreover, employees who work in a negative work environment are more likely to experience stress, burnout, and other health problems, which can lead to increased absenteeism and decreased overall productivity.

Another significant financial implication of negative leadership is increased turnover. Negative leaders often create an environment in which employees are not valued, and this can lead to high levels of employee turnover. The costs associated with hiring and training new employees can be substantial, and high turnover rates can quickly erode an organisation's bottom line. Moreover, when employees leave, they take their knowledge, skills, and experience with them, which can also have a negative impact on the organisation's performance.

Negative leadership can also impact an organisation's reputation and brand. When employees are not happy with their working environment, they are more likely to speak out and share their experiences, both within and outside the organisation. This can harm the company's reputation and brand, making it difficult to attract new employees and customers.

Additionally, negative leadership can lead to legal and regulatory issues, as well as increased litigation costs. For example, if a leader engages in unethical behaviour, such as discrimination, the organisation could face significant legal and financial consequences.

Negative leadership can have serious financial implications for organisations. Decreased productivity, increased turnover, damaged reputation and brand, and legal and regulatory issues can all impact an organisation's bottom line. As such, it is critical for organisations to identify negative leaders and take steps to address their behaviour. This may involve providing leadership training, implementing new policies and procedures, or replacing negative leaders with more effective leaders. By doing so, organisations can create a positive work environment, increase employee morale and productivity, and protect their bottom line.

One of the most significant financial implications of negative leadership is decreased productivity. According to a study conducted by the Harvard Business Review, ineffective leaders can decrease employee engagement and productivity by up to 30%. This can result in a significant loss in revenue for organisations.

Another financial implication of negative leadership is high turnover rates. Negative leaders can create a toxic working environment that leads to high turnover rates. This can be costly for organisations as the cost of replacing an employee can range from 50-200% of their annual salary.

Additionally, negative leadership can also decrease employee morale and motivation, which can result in decreased innovation and problem-solving capabilities. This can lead to decreased competitiveness and reduced market share for organisations.

Negative leadership can also result in legal issues and lawsuits. For example, if a leader engages in discriminatory or harassing behaviour, they may face legal action, which can result in significant financial losses for the organisation.

The financial implications of negative leadership can be significant and far-reaching. Organisations can suffer decreased productivity, high turnover rates, decreased competitiveness, and legal issues, all of which can result in significant financial losses. It is, therefore, crucial for organisations to invest in positive leadership and promote a culture of good leadership practices.

Negative leadership can have far-reaching consequences that go beyond monetary implications. In this section, we will explore the other consequences of negative leadership in detail.

First and foremost, negative leadership can result in a demotivated workforce. Leaders who are authoritarian, manipulative, or abusive can create a toxic work environment where employees feel undervalued, unappreciated, and unsupported. This can lead to a lack of motivation, decreased productivity, and an increase in absenteeism and turnover. A demotivated workforce can also result in a decline in the quality of work produced, which can lead to a decrease in customer satisfaction.

Secondly, negative leadership can result in a lack of trust and respect within an organization. Leaders who are dishonest, unreliable, or inconsistent can damage the trust and respect that employees have for them. This can result in a breakdown of communication, a lack of collaboration, and a lack of teamwork. In turn, this can lead to a decline in the overall effectiveness of the organization and can make it difficult to achieve common goals.

Thirdly, negative leadership can result in a lack of innovation and creativity. Leaders who are resistant to change or who do not encourage new ideas and experimentation can stifle innovation and creativity within an organization. This can result in a lack of competitiveness, a decrease in market share, and an inability to keep up with the changing needs and demands of customers.

Fourthly, negative leadership can result in a decline in the mental health and wellbeing of employees. Leaders who create a toxic work environment can lead to increased levels of stress, anxiety, and depression in employees. This can result in decreased levels of job satisfaction, a decrease in productivity, and an increase in absenteeism and turnover.

Lastly, negative leadership can result in reputational damage for an organization. Leaders who participate in unethical or illegal practices can damage the reputation of the organization, resulting in a loss of trust and confidence from customers, stakeholders, and the general public. This can result in a decline in revenue, difficulty in attracting new customers, and can even lead to legal action against the organization.

Another consequence of negative leadership is the erosion of trust between leaders and their employees. When leaders fail to follow through on their promises, or engage in behavior that is perceived as unfair or unethical, employees may lose trust in their leaders. This can lead to decreased morale, low job satisfaction, and decreased engagement in their work.

Negative leadership can also impact an organization's reputation and its ability to attract and retain top talent. If word gets out that an organization has a toxic work environment or negative leadership, it can deter potential employees from joining the organization or cause current employees to leave. This can result in a talent drain, leaving the organization with less qualified and less engaged employees.

Ultimately, negative leadership can have far-reaching consequences that extend beyond the bottom line. It can impact the well-being of employees, erode trust, damage an organization's reputation, and hinder its ability to attract and retain top talent. Therefore, it is important for leaders to prioritize positive leadership practices that promote employee well-being, build trust, and foster a healthy work environment.

All the consequences of negative leadership mentioned are only a few examples from the corporate world. It can expand to personal, social, and martial life on a far larger scale, requiring encyclopedias to go through them one by one. Leaders must understand the importance of good leadership and the impact it has on the organization and its employees. It is essential to develop and promote a positive leadership style that fosters a healthy work environment, encourages trust and respect, fosters innovation and creativity, and values the wellbeing of employees.

PART-25

STARTING OF LEADERSHIP

L eadership is a critical aspect of society that has the power to shape organisations, communities, and individuals. But where does leadership begin? How does someone become a leader? These are important questions that have been studied and discussed for decades. In this section, we will explore the origins of leadership and examine how it starts and develops.

Leadership starts with self-awareness. Leaders must first understand their own values, beliefs, and motivations before they can effectively lead others. Self-awareness involves a deeper understanding of one's strengths, weaknesses, and personal qualities. Leaders who are self-aware are better equipped to identify their own leadership style, understand their impact on others, and make informed decisions for their organisation.

Leadership also starts with personal growth and development. Leaders who invest in their own growth and learning are better equipped to lead effectively. Personal growth can involve pursuing new hobbies, learning new skills, reading books, attending workshops, or engaging in any other activity that broadens one's knowledge and skills. A leader who invests in personal growth is more confident, adaptable, and innovative and is better equipped to lead others.

Leadership begins with taking action. Leaders who take the initiative and take action are better equipped to lead effectively. Taking action involves taking risks, making decisions, and solving problems. Leaders who take action are not afraid to step outside their comfort zones and make a difference in their communities, organisations, and personal lives.

Leadership starts with relationships. Leaders who have strong relationships with others are better equipped to lead effectively. Relationships involve building trust, communication, and understanding others. Leaders who nurture their relationships are more likely to have a supportive network of friends, family, and colleagues and are better equipped to lead others.

Leadership starts with making a positive impact. Leaders who make a positive impact on others are better equipped to lead effectively. Making a positive impact involves serving others, making a difference in the lives of others, and contributing to the greater good. Leaders who make a positive impact are more likely to inspire others, build trust, and have a lasting impact on the world.

Leadership starts with self-awareness, personal growth, taking action, relationships, and making a positive impact. Leaders who invest in these areas are better equipped to lead effectively and have a lasting impact on the world. By focusing on these areas, anyone can develop leadership skills and make a difference in the lives of others.

Leadership is a crucial aspect of organisational and social life, and it plays a significant role in shaping the success of organisations and communities. The development of leadership skills is closely linked to the structure and hierarchy of organisations and societies. In this section, we will explore the relationship between leadership development and organisational and social hierarchy and how they impact each other.

Organisational Hierarchy: Organisations are typically structured in a hierarchical manner, with different levels of leadership and management. The structure of an organisation often determines the opportunities for leadership development and the responsibilities of leaders. For example, a leader in a higher position within the organisation may have more opportunities for professional growth and is responsible for leading a larger team. On the other hand, leaders in lower positions may have fewer opportunities for leadership development but may still have a significant impact on their team and the organisation as a whole.

The development of leadership skills within an organisation is often tied to the opportunities for career progression. For instance, a leader who is able to demonstrate their leadership skills at one level of the organisation may be promoted to a higher position and given greater responsibilities. This progression can lead to further opportunities for leadership development and professional growth.

Social Hierarchy: In a similar manner, social hierarchy can also impact the development of leadership skills. The opportunities for leadership development may vary based on one's social status, race, gender, and other factors. For example, someone from a lower socio-economic background may have fewer opportunities for leadership development and may face more obstacles in pursuing a leadership role.

On the other hand, someone from a higher socio-economic background may have more access to resources and opportunities for leadership development.

The development of leadership skills is closely linked to the structure and hierarchy of organisations and societies. Organisations and social structures can either support or hinder the development of one's leadership skills, and it is, therefore, important to understand this relationship in order to create opportunities for leadership development for all individuals. By promoting diversity and inclusion in leadership and creating equal opportunities for leadership development, organisations and societies can ensure that they are fostering the growth and success of their leaders.

PART-26

MEASURE LEADERSHIP EFFECTIVENESS

Effective leadership can drive positive outcomes, including increased productivity, employee satisfaction, and organisational growth. However, evaluating the effectiveness of leadership can be a challenging task, as it involves assessing multiple complex factors. In this section, we will explore the key considerations for measuring the effectiveness of leadership, including both objective and subjective metrics.

Objective Metrics: Objective metrics refer to the tangible and quantifiable aspects of leadership effectiveness. These metrics can provide valuable insights into the performance of leaders and the impact they have on their organisations. Some of the key objective metrics for measuring leadership effectiveness include:

Financial Performance: Financial performance is often seen as a primary indicator of organisational success and can provide a valuable metric for assessing leadership effectiveness. This can include metrics such as revenue growth, profit margins, and return on investment.

Productivity: Productivity metrics can also provide a valuable indicator of the impact of leadership on the effectiveness of individuals and teams. This can include metrics such as output per hour, customer satisfaction scores, and employee engagement levels.

Employee Satisfaction: Employee satisfaction is a critical metric for measuring leadership effectiveness, as it provides insights into the working environment, employee morale, and the effectiveness of leadership in fostering positive relationships. Employee satisfaction metrics can include employee turnover rates, absenteeism, and exit interviews.

Subjective Metrics: Subjective metrics refer to the perceptions and opinions of individuals regarding leadership effectiveness. These metrics can provide valuable insights into the impact of leadership on employees and other stakeholders. Some of the key subjective metrics for measuring leadership effectiveness include:

Leadership Style: Leadership style can have a significant impact on employee satisfaction and motivation. Assessing the leadership style of an individual can provide valuable insights into their effectiveness as a leader.

Employee Feedback: Employee feedback can provide valuable insights into the impact of leadership on the working environment, employee morale, and the effectiveness of leadership in fostering positive relationships. Employee feedback can be obtained through regular employee surveys, focus groups, or exit interviews.

Perceptions of Organisational Culture: Organisational culture is a critical aspect of leadership, as it sets the tone for the behaviour and attitudes of employees. Assessing the perceptions of organisational culture can provide valuable insights into the impact of leadership on the overall working environment.

Measuring the effectiveness of leadership is a complex task that involves considering both objective and subjective metrics. By focusing on financial performance, productivity, employee satisfaction, leadership style, employee feedback, and organisational culture, leaders and organisations can gain valuable insights into the impact of their leadership and take action to drive positive outcomes.

Measuring the effectiveness of leadership in a social environment can be a challenging task, as the impact of leadership is often subjective and difficult to quantify. However, there are several tools and methodologies that can be used to evaluate the effectiveness of leaders in social environments, such as:

Surveys and questionnaires: Surveys and questionnaires can be used to gather data from stakeholders, such as employees, customers, and community members, about their perceptions of leadership. These tools can help to gauge the impact of leadership on morale, engagement, and satisfaction.

Key performance indicators (KPIs): KPIs are quantitative measures that can be used to track and evaluate the performance of a leader. For example, in a social environment, KPIs could include metrics such as volunteerism, community involvement, and charitable giving.

Focus groups: Focus groups bring together a small group of stakeholders to discuss their perceptions of leadership. This methodology can provide valuable insights into the impact of leadership on various stakeholders and can be particularly useful in gaining a deeper understanding of the impact of leadership on the community.

Case studies: Case studies are in-depth examinations of real-life situations and can be used to evaluate the effectiveness of leadership in a particular context. For example, a case study could examine the impact of a leader on a specific community or social issue.

360-degree feedback: 360-degree feedback is a tool that allows stakeholders, such as employees, colleagues, and community members, to provide feedback on the leadership skills and behaviours of a leader. This method can provide valuable insights into the impact of leadership on the organisation and the community.

Social media analysis: Social media platforms can be a valuable source of data on the impact of leadership in a social environment. Analysing the conversations and interactions taking place on social media platforms can provide insights into the perception of leadership among stakeholders and can highlight areas for improvement.

Measuring the effectiveness of leadership in a social environment requires a multi-faceted approach, utilizing a combination of qualitative and quantitative methods to gather data and gain a comprehensive understanding of the impact of leadership. By using the tools and methodologies outlined above, organisations and communities can evaluate the effectiveness of their leaders and take steps to improve leadership practices, which ultimately leads to a more positive social environment.

The question of who determines if a person is a leader or not depends on many factors, including personal and organisational culture, social and historical context, and individual interpretation and experiences. However, there are some general factors that are often used to determine whether someone is a leader, and these factors can provide useful guidance for those seeking to understand this concept.

One of the most common approaches to determine if a person is a leader or not is based on their ability to influence others. This can be seen through the individual's ability to motivate, inspire, engage others, communicate effectively, and build relationships. This is often considered the most important characteristic of leadership and is often seen as the key factor that distinguishes leaders from non-leaders.

Another factor that is often used to determine if a person is a leader or not is their level of experience and expertise. This can be measured through a combination of education, training, and practical experience and is often seen as a key indicator of leadership potential. For example, someone who has extensive experience in a particular industry or field may be considered a leader in that area, while someone with a more general background may not be seen in the same light.

Finally, leadership can also be determined based on personal characteristics, such as intelligence, creativity, integrity, and emotional intelligence. These traits can help individuals build relationships and make decisions effectively, and these traits are often seen as key indicators of leadership potential. For example, a person who is able to think creatively and effectively manage their emotions may be seen as a strong leader, even if they lack experience or education in a particular field.

Determining if a person is a leader or not can be complex and subjective and often involves a combination of factors, including influence, experience, and personal characteristics. While there may not be a single answer to this question, understanding these general factors can provide useful guidance for those seeking to understand the concept of leadership and can help to shed light on the many different approaches that are used to evaluate and determine leadership effectiveness.

PART-27

LEADERSHIP AND COACHING

L eadership and coaching have been considered two complementary practices, and the relationship between these two fields is complex and multi-faceted. The development of leadership skills and practices has long been intertwined with the principles of coaching, and it is widely accepted that coaching can have a significant impact on the effectiveness of leadership.

Leadership is typically described as the ability to inspire, motivate, and guide a group of individuals toward a common goal. On the other hand, coaching is often defined as a process of facilitating individual growth and development by helping individuals identify their strengths and weaknesses, setting goals, and providing support and guidance as they work towards achieving their objectives.

While these two practices may seem distinct, they are interconnected and overlap in many important ways. For example, a coach can provide valuable guidance and support to individuals who are in leadership positions, helping them to overcome challenges, develop new skills, and improve their leadership abilities. At the same time, effective leaders must possess many of the same skills and qualities as effective coaches, such as active listening, empathy, the ability to inspire and motivate, and the ability to provide clear and constructive feedback.

In many organisations, leadership development programs often incorporate coaching as an important component. For example, executive coaches may work with leaders to help them identify areas for improvement, develop new skills, and gain greater self-awareness. This type of coaching can have a significant impact on a leader's ability to be more effective, as it helps them understand their strengths and limitations and provides opportunities for them to learn and grow.

Another area where the relationship between leadership and coaching is evident is in the field of team development. Effective leaders must be able to build and lead high-performing teams, and coaching can play an important role in this process. For example, a coach can help team members understand their roles and responsibilities, communicate effectively with each other, and develop their problem-solving and decision-making skills.

The relationship between leadership and coaching is complex and multi-faceted, and these two practices are inextricably linked. Effective leaders must possess many of the same skills and qualities as effective coaches, and coaching can also have a significant impact on the effectiveness of leadership. By leveraging the principles of coaching, leaders can improve their abilities, build stronger teams, and have a greater impact on their organisations and communities.

Developing coaching skills for leadership can greatly enhance one's ability to lead effectively and bring about a positive change in their organisation or community. Coaching is a process of helping individuals identify and achieve their goals, and it requires a unique set of skills and mindset that is often different from traditional leadership approaches. Here are several ways to develop coaching skills for leadership:

Mindset Shift: One of the most important steps in developing coaching skills is to shift your mindset from a traditional leadership mindset to a coaching mindset. This involves moving from a directive approach, where you tell others what to do, to a collaborative approach, where you help others find their own solutions.

Active Listening: Coaching requires you to be a great listener and understand what the other person is saying, both verbally and non-verbally. This requires focusing your attention on the person and avoiding distractions, as well as reflecting on what you have heard and rephrasing it back to the person to ensure that you have understood.

Questioning Techniques: As a coach, you need to be able to ask questions that are thought-provoking to help the person reflect on their situation. Open-ended questions are a great way to get people thinking, while closed questions can help you gather specific information.

Goal-Setting: One of the key elements of coaching is goal-setting. As a coach, you need to help individuals identify their goals and develop a plan to achieve them. This involves setting realistic and achievable goals, breaking them down into smaller steps, and creating a timeline for their completion.

Empathy: To be an effective coach, you need to be able to understand and connect with people on a deeper level. **Encouragement:** Encouragement is a crucial part of coaching. As a coach, you need to be able to provide support and motivate the person to take action and move forward, even when they face challenges or obstacles.

Feedback: As a coach, it's important to provide regular and constructive feedback to help the person make progress and stay on track. Feedback should be specific, objective, and focused on behaviour and actions that can be improved.

Developing coaching skills for leadership requires a shift in mindset, a focus on active listening, effective questioning, goal-setting, empathy, encouragement, and providing regular feedback. With these skills in place, leaders can create a supportive environment for their team and help them achieve their goals, bringing about positive change and growth in their organisation or community.

Coaching is an important aspect of leadership that helps individuals to grow and develop in their careers. It involves providing guidance, support, and giving feedback to help individuals identify their strengths and weaknesses, set goals, and create action plans to achieve their aspirations. However, there comes a point when coaching should stop.

One of the factors that determine when to stop coaching is the achievement of goals. When the individual has successfully accomplished the goals set in their coaching plan, it may be time to end the coaching relationship. This signifies that the coaching has been effective in supporting the individual in reaching their desired outcome. At this point, the individual should have developed the skills and confidence to continue on their own.

Another factor to consider is the individual's level of growth and development. If the individual has reached a level where they have fully developed the skills and competencies necessary for their role, it may be time to stop coaching. In such cases, continuing coaching may become redundant and not add much value to the individual's growth.

The coaching relationship should also be re-evaluated if the individual is no longer benefiting from it. If the individual is not actively engaged in the coaching process and is not making any significant progress, it may be time to stop coaching. In such cases, the coach may need to re-evaluate the coaching approach and find a more effective method to support the individual's growth and development.

Lastly, the end of a coaching relationship may also be due to changes in the individual's circumstances. For example, if the individual changes jobs or roles, the coaching may no longer be relevant to their current situation. In such cases, the coaching relationship may need to be terminated, and a new coaching plan needs to be developed for the individual's new role.

Coaching relationship is an important aspect of leadership that should be carefully considered. Coaching should only continue if it provides value and supports the individual's growth and development. When coaching is no longer effective or relevant, it may be time to stop and move on to other developmental opportunities.

In social life, coaching can be used to develop the leadership skills of individuals, helping them to lead themselves and others more effectively.

The first step in developing a coaching relationship in the context of leadership is to understand the role that coaching plays in this process. Coaching is a supportive and collaborative approach to learning that helps individuals to identify their strengths and weaknesses, set goals, and develop the skills and strategies needed to achieve those goals. It is a process that is often used to help leaders identify their leadership styles and develop the skills they need to be effective in their roles.

In the context of leadership, coaching can be used to help individuals identify the areas in which they need to improve, as well as the strengths and skills that they already possess. This can help them build a stronger foundation for their leadership journey, as well as provide them with the tools and strategies they need to be successful. Additionally, coaching can be used to help individuals identify the challenges and obstacles that they may face in their leadership role and develop the skills and strategies needed to overcome these challenges.

One of the key benefits of coaching in the context of leadership is that it helps create a supportive and collaborative environment where individuals can learn from one another and build strong relationships. This is particularly important in social life, where leaders often need to build strong relationships with others in order to be effective. Coaching can help create a safe and supportive space where leaders can share their experiences, learn from one another, and grow together.

Coaching is an essential aspect of leadership, and the relationship between coaching and leadership is an important one that can help create stronger and more effective leaders. Whether in the context of social life or in a more formal setting, coaching can be used to help individuals identify their strengths and weaknesses, set goals, and develop the skills and strategies needed to achieve those goals. Ultimately, coaching can help individuals become more confident, effective, and impactful leaders.

Leadership coaching has become a popular tool in recent years, as organisations and individuals alike have come to recognise its ability to drive improvement in a variety of areas. This type of coaching is designed to help leaders hone their skills, overcome challenges, and achieve their goals more effectively. And while the benefits of leadership coaching are well documented, it is not always clear how these benefits are being realised in practice.

To understand the positive impact of coaching during the process of leadership, it is helpful to look at the results of studies and surveys that have been conducted on this topic. For example, a recent study found that organisations that invested in leadership coaching experienced significant improvements in areas such as employee engagement, productivity, and financial performance. Specifically, the study found that companies that offered leadership coaching to their employees saw a 14% increase in employee engagement and a 12% improvement in productivity.

Another study found that companies that offered leadership coaching to their employees were more likely to see improvements in financial performance, with a reported 20%

increase in profits. This finding is particularly significant, as it suggests that leadership coaching can not only improve the day-to-day operations of a company but can also have a real impact on its bottom line.

Of course, the benefits of leadership coaching are not limited to the workplace. In fact, many individuals have reported that leadership coaching has had a positive impact on their personal lives as well. For example, a recent survey found that individuals who participated in leadership coaching reported increased self-awareness, improved communication skills, and enhanced relationships with others.

While these statistics demonstrate the clear and tangible benefits of leadership coaching, they only tell part of the story. To truly understand the impact of coaching on leadership, it is also important to look at the process itself.

Leadership coaching typically involves working with a coach to identify and address specific areas of improvement. This may include improving communication skills, overcoming challenges in the workplace, or developing more effective strategies for leading a team. Throughout the coaching process, the coach provides guidance and support, helping the individual to make real and lasting changes.

The benefits of this process are numerous and go far beyond the specific skills and strategies that are learned. For example, many individuals who participate in leadership coaching report an increase in self-confidence, a better understanding of their strengths and weaknesses, and a greater sense of personal empowerment.

In addition, leadership coaching can help individuals develop a more nuanced understanding of the world around them and of the complex relationships that exist within organisations and communities. Through the coaching process, leaders are able to gain a better understanding of their own motivations and the motivations of others, and they learn to use this understanding to build stronger and more effective relationships.

Overall, the positive impact of coaching on the process of leadership is clear. Whether in the workplace or in our personal lives, leadership coaching can help individuals become more effective leaders and creates a positive impact on the world around them.

PART-28

COURAGE AND HUMANITY IN LEADERSHIP

Courage and humanity are two important aspects of leadership that are closely related to effective leadership. Courage refers to the willingness to take risks and face challenges, even in the face of fear and uncertainty. On the other hand, humanity refers to the qualities of compassion, empathy, and kindness that are essential for building positive relationships with others.

In leadership, courage plays a critical role in helping leaders make tough decisions, especially in times of crisis or uncertainty. A leader who is courageous is able to inspire others to follow and support them, even in difficult situations. For example, a courageous leader may choose to take a stand against an unjust policy or decision, even if it means facing consequences such as criticism or backlash.

At the same time, humanity is equally important in leadership. A leader who is compassionate and empathetic is better equipped to understand the needs and concerns of others and build positive relationships with team members, stakeholders, and other individuals. This can help foster a positive and supportive working environment where team members feel valued and respected and are more likely to be productive and engaged.

The connection between courage and humanity in leadership is that both aspects are essential for effective and inspiring leadership. Courage helps leaders make tough decisions and lead by example, while humanity helps leaders build positive relationships and foster a supportive working environment. Both of these qualities are critical for leaders who want to inspire and empower others to reach their full potential.

Leadership is a complex and multi-faceted concept that involves a number of key traits, such as courage and humanity. Both of these traits can have both positive and negative impacts on leadership, depending on how they are used. On one hand, courage and humanity can help leaders to effectively connect with and inspire their followers, creating a sense of trust and loyalty that can drive success. On the other hand, if not used wisely, these traits can also lead to a number of downsides, such as emotional burnout, ethical missteps, and a lack of effectiveness.

One of the biggest pros of incorporating courage and humanity into leadership is that it allows leaders to effectively connect with and motivate their followers. For example, a leader who is courageous and empathetic is often able to inspire others to work towards a common goal, even in the face of adversity. This can be particularly beneficial in social and emotional environments, where individuals may need to be lifted up and encouraged in order to achieve success.

However, there are also a number of potential downsides to incorporating courage and humanity into leadership. For example, leaders who are too empathetic and compassionate can become emotionally exhausted, which can ultimately undermine their effectiveness. Additionally, leaders who are too courageous may be more likely to make impulsive or un-ethical decisions, which can lead to negative consequences for themselves and their organisations.

For example, courage in leadership can be both a strength and a weakness. On one hand, a leader with the courage to take risks and make bold decisions can inspire confidence and motivation in their team. On the other hand, a leader who lacks caution or proper judgement can make costly mistakes, leading to negative consequences for the organisation and its stakeholders.

Similarly, a leader who embodies humanity and empathy can create a positive and supportive working environment, foster stronger relationships with employees, and make difficult decisions with consideration for the people involved. However, a leader who places too much emphasis on personal relationships or becomes too emotionally involved can struggle to make tough decisions, prioritise goals, and maintain objectivity.

Therefore, it's important for leaders to strike a balance between courage and humanity, recognizing the potential benefits and drawbacks of each aspect and striving to use these traits in a manner that is both effective and responsible. This can be achieved through a combination of self-awareness, mindfulness, and intentional decision-making.

Overall, the relationship between courage and humanity in leadership is complex and multifaceted, with both aspects having positive and negative implications. Effective leaders must therefore balance these traits in order to achieve success, both for themselves and for their organisation

PART-29

PSYCHOLOGY OF LEADERSHIP

There are many factors that contribute to a person's ability to be an effective leader, including their personality, emotional intelligence, and life experiences.

One of the key elements of the psychology of leadership is the role of personality. Research has shown that certain personality traits are more commonly found in leaders than in the general population. For example, leaders tend to be more extraverted and confident, with a strong sense of self-efficacy and a high degree of emotional stability. They are also often optimistic and open to new ideas, which helps them to think creatively and take risks.

Another important aspect of the psychology of leadership is emotional intelligence. Leaders with high levels of emotional intelligence are better able to build strong relationships with their followers, to communicate effectively, and to navigate through complex emotional situations. They are also better able to maintain their composure and make clear decisions, even under pressure.

In addition to personality and emotional intelligence, the life experiences of a leader can also have a significant impact on their effectiveness. For example, leaders who have faced challenges and overcome obstacles in their personal or professional lives often have a better understanding of the difficulties that their followers may be facing and a greater ability to motivate and support them.

Despite the many factors that contribute to the psychology of leadership, it is important to remember that there is no single "leadership personality." Effective leaders come in many shapes and sizes, and what works for one person may not work for another. Ultimately, the best way to develop your leadership skills is to engage in ongoing self-reflection and professional development and seek out opportunities to learn from experienced leaders and coaches.

Studies have found that certain personality traits are associated with effective leadership, such as emotional stability, extraversion, agreeableness, and openness to experience. For example, emotional stability is important for leaders because it allows them to remain calm and composed under stress, which is a critical component of effective leadership. Similarly, extraversion is important for leaders because it allows them to be confident and assertive, which can help them to get their message across and motivate others.

In terms of financial impact, research has found that effective leadership can have a significant impact on the financial performance of organisations. For example, one study found that companies with high-performing CEOs had an average return on equity of 17%, compared to just 9% for companies with low-performing CEOs. This demonstrates the importance of understanding the psychological factors that influence leadership and the potential financial rewards that can result from effective leadership.

Another important aspect of the psychology of leadership is the impact of cognitive biases on decision making. Research has found that leaders are prone to a number of biases, such as the confirmation bias, which is the tendency to only consider information that supports one's existing beliefs. This can have a negative impact on decision making and lead to poor outcomes.

Finally, the role of motivation in leadership is also an important area of focus in the psychology of leadership. Research has found that leaders who are motivated by a sense of purpose and mission are more likely to be effective and likely to achieve better results. This is because they are driven by a clear sense of what they want to accomplish and are more focused on achieving their goals.

The psychology of leadership is a complex and fascinating area of study that has the potential to help us better understand and improve the way we lead others. Whether you are a seasoned leader or just starting out on your leadership journey, understanding the factors that influence your effectiveness as a leader can help you to be more confident, effective, and impactful in your work.

PART-30

INNOVATIVE
LEADERS

Innovation is a crucial aspect of modern-day business and society, and it is the leaders who drive change and create new solutions for the future. Innovative leaders are individuals who have a forward-thinking mindset, an entrepreneurial spirit, and the courage to take risks. They are often the catalysts for change and play a vital role in shaping the future of their organisations and industries.

Innovative leaders are creative thinkers who are not afraid to challenge the status quo and push boundaries. They possess a deeper understanding of their respective industries and are able to identify new opportunities and trends. They are constantly seeking out new ways to solve problems and improve processes, and they are willing to experiment and test new ideas. This mindset of continuous improvement sets them apart from traditional leaders who may be more risk-averse and focused on maintaining the status quo.

Innovation is not just about developing new products or services, and it also involves creating new business models, disrupting established industries, and finding new ways to solve problems. Innovative leaders understand that success requires taking calculated risks, and they are willing to put their reputations on the line to bring about change.

Innovative leaders also understand the importance of collaboration and teamwork. They recognise that the best ideas often come from diverse perspectives, and they encourage open and honest dialogue. They create a culture of innovation by fostering an environment of trust, transparency, and collaboration.

In addition to their innovative mindset, innovative leaders are also skilled communicators. They are able to articulate their vision and inspire others to get behind their ideas. They are charismatic and are able to rally their teams around a common goal.

One of the key factors that set innovative leaders apart from traditional leaders is their willingness to embrace technology. They understand the potential of technology to drive change and are quick to adopt new technologies that can help them achieve their goals. They are not afraid to embrace new tools and platforms, and they understand how to use technology to reach new audiences and bring about change.

A real-life example of an innovative leader is Elon Musk. He is the CEO and co-founder of SpaceX, Tesla, Neuralink, and The Boring Company. He is known for his ability to disrupt traditional industries, such as space travel and automotive, and bring new and innovative products to market.

Under Musk's leadership, SpaceX became the first privately-funded company to send a spacecraft to the International Space Station and also launch and land reusable rockets. Tesla, on the other hand, is revolutionizing the automotive industry by producing electric cars with superior performance and range compared to conventional vehicles.

The impact of Musk's innovative leadership can be seen in the financial success of his companies. According to Forbes, as of January 2023, Musk's net worth was over $200 billion, making him one of the richest people in the world. Furthermore, Tesla's market value has grown to over $800 billion, making it one of the most valuable car companies in the world.

In conclusion, innovative leaders like Elon Musk have the ability to create significant change and bring new solutions to problems. Their leadership skills are in high demand and have the potential to bring about financial success for their companies and themselves. By observing and learning from innovative leaders like Musk, aspiring leaders can develop the skills and mindset needed to become innovative themselves.

In today's fast-paced and constantly changing world, innovation has become an essential aspect of leadership. Embracing innovation in leadership not only enables leaders to adapt to new challenges and opportunities but also helps organisations to stay ahead of the curve and remain competitive. However, many leaders struggle to embrace innovation and may be intimidated by the uncertainty and risk associated with it. In this section, we will explore the steps leaders can take to embrace innovation in their leadership style and create a culture of innovation within their organisations.

Embrace a Growth Mindset: The first step to embracing innovation is to have a growth mindset. Leaders with a growth mindset believe that their abilities and skills can be developed through effort and experience. They are open to learning new things and are not afraid of failure. This mindset allows them to embrace innovation and take calculated risks.

Encourage Creativity and Risk-Taking: Leaders must create an environment that encourages creativity and risk-taking. This means providing resources, support, and opportunities for employees to experiment and come up with new ideas. Leaders must also establish a culture where employees feel comfortable sharing their thoughts and taking risks, even if their ideas may not be successful.

Foster Collaboration: Leaders must foster collaboration and teamwork within their organisations. Innovation often occurs when individuals with different perspectives and skills work together to find creative solutions. By encouraging collaboration, leaders can tap into the collective creativity of their teams and come up with innovative ideas that they may not have thought of on their own.

Stay Up-to-Date with Industry Trends: Leaders must stay up-to-date with industry trends and technological advancements. This means attending conferences, networking events, and reading industry publications to stay well informed of the latest developments. Leaders who are knowledgeable about the latest trends are better equipped to embrace innovation and make informed decisions.

Empower Employees: Leaders must empower their employees to take ownership of their work and make decisions. This means giving them the autonomy to make decisions, solve problems and take risks. By empowering employees, leaders can tap into their creativity and generate new ideas that can drive innovation.

In conclusion, embracing innovation in leadership is crucial for organisations to remain competitive and stay ahead of the curve. By embracing a growth mindset, encouraging creativity and risk-taking, fostering collaboration, staying up-to-date with industry trends, and empowering employees, leaders can create a culture of innovation that drives success. By taking these steps, leaders can position themselves and their organisations for success in a rapidly changing world.

PART-31

SKILLS
AND HABIT
ADAPTATION

The concept of habit change and adaptation is widely discussed in the fields of psychology, self-improvement, and leadership. One popular approach to habit change is the 66-day habit change theory, which suggests that it takes approximately 66 days to form a new habit. This theory is based on the idea that habits are formed through repeated actions that eventually become automatic, taking less and less conscious effort over time.

The 66-day habit change theory is often used as a benchmark for individuals seeking to form new habits, such as exercise routines, healthy eating habits, or time management techniques. According to the theory, if an individual repeats a specific behaviour every day for 66 days, that behaviour will become a habit and will be easier to maintain over time.

However, it is important to note that the actual duration for habit change and adaptation can vary from person to person and can depend on a variety of factors, such as the complexity of the habit, the individual's personal motivation, and environmental factors. Some research suggests that it can take anywhere from 18 to 254 days to form a new habit, with the average being 66 days.

When it comes to developing new skills in adulthood, the duration for habit change and adaptation can also vary. However, research suggests that the adult brain is capable of learning and adapting new skills throughout its lifespan. As a result, the process of habit change and adaptation in adults can be more efficient compared to children who are still developing their cognitive and motor skills.

It is also important to consider that the first seven years of a child's life are crucial for developing the foundation of habits and behaviours that will influence their future. During this time, children are more susceptible to habit formation and are more likely to adopt behaviours and habits that are modelled by the adults in their lives.

Finally, it is worth mentioning that there is a phenomenon known as "shocked adaptation," which refers to the rapid formation of new habits or behaviours in response to a sudden change or shock in the individual's environment. For example, a sudden injury that limits physical activity can lead to the rapid formation of new habits and behaviours focused on rehabilitation and recovery.

The duration of habit change and adaptation can vary widely depending on a variety of factors, including the individual's age, the complexity of the habit, and environmental factors. The 66-day habit change theory is often used as a benchmark, but it is important to understand that habit formation is a complex process that can take varying amounts of time and effort. Nevertheless, with a clearer understanding of habit change and adaptation, individuals can make conscious efforts to develop new skills and habits to improve their lives and reach their goals.

Shocked adaptation or habit disruptive is a technique used to quickly modify habits and bring about change in a short amount of time. The concept is based on the idea that, in order to break a habit, a person needs to experience a significant, emotional event that acts as a catalyst for change. This event can be positive or negative, but it must be strong enough to disrupt the normal patterns of behaviour and prompt the individual to re-evaluate their habits.

In the context of habit change, the 66-day rule is often used as a rough estimate of the time it takes to form a new habit. This timeline is based on a study by plastic surgeon Maxwell Maltz, who observed that it took his patients approximately 21 days to get used to a new physical change, such as a prosthetic limb. However, this concept has been challenged and updated, with more recent research suggesting that it may take anywhere from 18 to 254 days to form a new habit, depending on the individual and the behaviour being changed.

For adults, the duration of habit change can vary greatly depending on a number of factors. Some habits may be easier to change than others, and the length of time it takes to form a new habit can depend on the individual's motivation, the complexity of the behaviour, and the support available to help them stick to their new habits. It is also important to note that some habits may require a significant investment of time and effort in order to change, while others may be modified relatively easily.

One of the key factors in successful habit change is the use of shock or a significant event that acts as a catalyst for change. This can be a positive event, such as a promotion or a new relationship, or a negative event, such as a health crisis or a financial setback. The shock acts as a wake-up call, prompting the individual to re-evaluate their habits and take action to make changes in their lives.

Habit change and adaptation are critical aspects of effective leadership, particularly in the military space, where success is often determined by a team's ability to operate effectively and efficiently in high-pressure and fast-paced environments. In the military, leaders must continuously adapt to new situations, technologies, and strategies, and the process of habit change is a crucial part of this evolution.

The military provides a unique and challenging environment for habit change, as soldiers are often called upon to perform physically, mentally, and emotionally demanding tasks in extreme conditions. This requires a strong foundation of discipline, training, and focus, all of which are built and maintained through consistent habit formation. The process of habit change in the military is, therefore, a key aspect of leadership development, as leaders must be able to identify the habits that need to be changed, develop new habits, and then ensure that these new habits are ingrained in the team.

One approach to habit change in the military is the "shocked adaptation" method, which involves rapidly changing a person's environment in order to create a sense of shock and further disrupt existing habits. This is done with the goal of rapidly creating new habits that are more aligned with the goals and objectives of the military organisation. For example, a leader might reorganise a team's structure, change the way tasks are assigned, or provide new equipment to encourage new habits to form.

Another key factor in habit change in the military is the duration of time required for adults to adapt to new skills. This can vary depending on a number of factors, including the individual's age, experience, and level of motivation. However, research suggests that, on average, it takes an adult approximately 66 days to form a new habit. This time frame can be shortened or lengthened based on the difficulty of the task and the individual's level of commitment.

The process of habit change and adaptation is an important aspect of leadership development in the military. Leaders must be able to identify the habits that need to be changed, develop new habits, and then ensure that these new habits are ingrained in their team. The use of the "shocked adaptation" and the understanding of the duration required for adult habit change can be useful tools in the process of leadership development and habit change in the military.

The concept of shocked adaptation or habit disruptive is a powerful tool for individuals looking to change their habits. While the 66-day rule is a rough estimate of the time it takes to form a new habit, the actual length of time can vary greatly depending on the individual and the behaviour being changed. However, by using a shock or a significant event as a catalyst for change, individuals can quickly and effectively modify their habits and bring about positive changes in their lives.

Habit change is a complex and multi-layered process that requires dedication, determination, and discipline. The process of habit change can be broken down into several key stages, including awareness, motivation, planning, execution, and evaluation.

The first stage of habit change is awareness. This is the stage where individuals become aware of the habit they wish to change and why they want to change it. They may become aware of the habit through self-reflection, feedback from others, or by observing the impact, the habit is having on their lives. Awareness is a crucial first step as it provides the foundation for the motivation to change.

The second stage of habit change is motivation. This is the stage where individuals are motivated to change the habit and make it a priority in their lives. Motivation can come from a variety of sources, such as a desire to improve their health, relationships, or personal growth. The motivation to change is what drives individuals to take action and start the process of habit change.

The third stage of habit change is planning. This is the stage where individuals create a plan to change the habit. They may choose to use strategies such as goal-setting, tracking progress, or seeking support from others. Planning helps individuals to be prepared for the challenges they may face during the habit change process.

The fourth stage of habit change is execution. This is the stage where individuals put their plan into action and start the process of changing the habit. It is important for individuals to be patient, persistent, and consistent in their efforts to change the habit. This stage may be challenging, and individuals may face setbacks and obstacles, but the key is to stay motivated and keep moving forward.

The final stage of habit change is evaluation. This is the stage where individuals reflect on their progress and evaluate their success. They may use tools such as self-reflection, feedback from others, or tracking their progress to determine their level of success. Evaluation helps individuals see their progress and make any necessary adjustments to their habit change plan.

The process of habit change can be broken down into several key stages, including awareness, motivation, planning, execution, and evaluation. By understanding and following these stages, individuals can successfully change their habits and achieve their goals.

PART-32

LEARNING LEADERSHIP FROM BARBERS

L eadership is a complex and multifaceted concept that has been the subject of study for many years. While leadership is commonly associated with politics, business, or the military, it can also be found in unexpected places, such as barbershops. In fact, barbers can provide valuable lessons and insights into the qualities and characteristics of effective leadership.

Barbers, like other service providers, must possess excellent communication skills to effectively understand the needs and desires of their clients. They must also be able to build trust and rapport with their clients in order to establish long-lasting relationships. These qualities are essential for effective leadership, as leaders must be able to communicate their vision and goals to their followers while also building trust and relationships with their team members.

Another important leadership quality that barbers must possess is the ability to manage their time and resources effectively. Barbering is a service-based industry that requires barbers to work under time constraints while also ensuring that they provide their clients with high-quality service. This requires barbers to be organised and efficient and to have a clear understanding of their workload and priorities. Similarly, leaders must be able to effectively manage their time and resources and prioritise their tasks in order to achieve their goals.

In addition to communication and time management skills, barbers must also be able to adapt and be flexible in their approach. In a barbershop, clients may have unique requests or needs that require the barber to adjust their approach. For example, a client may have a specific hair style in mind, or they may have a specific time constraint. The barber must be able to adapt their approach in order to accommodate these requests while still delivering high-quality service. Similarly, leaders must be able to adapt their approach and be flexible in order to respond to the changing needs and demands of their followers or team members.

Finally, barbers must also possess excellent interpersonal skills, as they must be able to engage with their clients in a friendly and welcoming manner. They must be able to listen to their clients and respond to their needs while also providing them with a comfortable and relaxing experience. Interpersonal skills are also essential for effective leadership, as leaders must be able to engage with their followers and team members and understand their needs and motivations.

One of the primary issues that affect barbers is a lack of communication and respect from leadership. This can take the form of not being informed about important decisions that affect their work, not having a voice in decision-making processes, or being subjected to demeaning or condescending behaviour. This type of leadership can create a negative working environment, which can impact barbers' job satisfaction, motivation, and overall performance.

Another issue that barbers face is a lack of support and resources from leadership. This can include not having access to the necessary tools, materials, or equipment to do their job effectively, not receiving adequate training or development opportunities, or not having a supportive workplace culture. This type of leadership can also lead to frustration, burnout, and a decrease in productivity.

In the context of leadership, these experiences can help to highlight the importance of open and respectful communication, as well as the need for leaders to provide the resources and support that employees need to succeed. When leaders listen to the concerns and experiences of their employees, they can gain valuable insights into what is important to them and what is needed to create a positive and productive work environment.

Moreover, effective leaders understand the value of providing development opportunities and investing in the growth and success of their employees. When leaders support their employees in this way, they are more likely to experience high levels of job satisfaction, motivation, and productivity. This type of leadership can create a virtuous cycle where employees are more engaged, motivated, and productive, which in turn, contributes to organisational success.

The experiences of barbers can provide valuable insights into leadership. The issues of a lack of communication, respect, and support can help highlight the importance of open communication, supportive resources, and employee development opportunities in creating a positive working environment and fostering organisational success. Effective leaders understand that the success of their organisations depends on the success of their employees, and they work to create an environment that supports and empowers them to succeed.

Barbers can provide valuable lessons and insights into the qualities and characteristics of effective leadership. By observing the communication, time management, adaptability, and interpersonal skills of barbers, we can gain a better understanding of the qualities that are essential for effective leadership. Whether in a barbershop or in a larger organisation, the principles of effective leadership remain the same, and by studying these principles, we can become better leaders ourselves.

Leadership is a critical aspect of life, and it has been found that the behaviour and habits of leaders can greatly impact the success of organisations and businesses. A barber, by definition, is someone who cuts and styles hair. However, barbers often play a much larger role in their communities as trusted confidantes and role models. They can also provide valuable lessons in leadership to anyone looking to improve their own leadership abilities.

One of the key habits that barbers exhibit is the ability to listen attentively. Barber shops are often bustling with customers, but despite the distractions, barbers are able to remain focused and engaged with each customer, listening to their needs and concerns. They understand the importance of active listening and are able to give their full attention to each customer, allowing them to connect with them on a personal level. This quality of active listening is critical for leaders as well, as it enables them to better understand the needs and concerns of those they lead and respond to their needs in an effective manner.

Another habit that barbers possess is the ability to be patient. In the barber shop, things can get busy, and customers may have to wait their turn. Barbers understand the importance of patience, and they do not let the stress of the situation get to them. They are able to remain calm and patient, providing a welcoming atmosphere for their customers. Leaders can also benefit from this habit, as it helps them maintain their composure in difficult situations and respond to challenges in a calm and rational manner.

Barbers also possess excellent interpersonal skills. In the barber shop, barbers must be able to interact with people from all walks of life and with varying personality types. They must be able to communicate effectively and understand the unique needs of each customer. This type of interpersonal skill is crucial for leaders as well, as it enables them to connect with and motivate their employees, building a positive and productive working environment.

Finally, barbers possess the ability to be adaptable. The barber shop is a fast-paced environment that requires quick thinking and the ability to change course quickly. Barbers must be able to adapt to different customer needs and unexpected situations in order to provide the best service possible. Leaders can also benefit from this habit, as it allows them to be nimble and responsive to changes in their industry, adapting to new challenges and opportunities as they arise.

To develop these habits and skills of leadership like barbers, one must start by becoming a more active listener. This can be achieved by putting away distractions, giving full attention to the person speaking, and asking questions to clarify understanding. Additionally, practicing patience through mindfulness and stress management techniques can help to cultivate this habit. Improving interpersonal skills can be accomplished through active communication and empathy training, while adaptability can be developed through continuous learning and embracing change.

Barbers can provide valuable lessons in leadership through their habits and skills. By developing these habits and skills, individuals can become more effective leaders, building positive and productive working environments that drive success. Whether in the barber shop or in the boardroom, these habits and skills will serve as a guide to successful leadership.

PART-33

CONSCIOUS, SUBCONSCIOUS, AND UNCONSCIOUS

The relationship between the conscious, subconscious, and unconscious mind with leadership is complex and multi-faceted. The conscious mind refers to the part of the mind that is aware and capable of thinking, problem-solving, and decision-making. The subconscious mind, on the other hand, is the part of the mind that controls habits, beliefs, and emotions. The unconscious mind, on the other hand, is the part of the mind that is beyond our awareness and is responsible for regulating functions such as breathing, heart rate, and digestion.

In the context of leadership, the conscious mind is the driving force behind our actions, thoughts, and decisions. It is the part of the mind that leaders rely on to make decisions, solve problems, and communicate with their team. However, the subconscious mind also plays a crucial role in leadership as it shapes our beliefs, attitudes, and habits. Our beliefs, attitudes, and habits can greatly impact our leadership style and the way we interact with others.

For example, if a leader has a subconscious belief that they are not good at public speaking, they may avoid public speaking opportunities and miss out on opportunities to communicate their vision and ideas. On the other hand, if a leader has a strong belief in their ability to inspire and motivate others, they are likely to exhibit confident and charismatic behaviour, which can have a positive impact on their team and organisation.

The unconscious mind also plays a role in leadership, as it is responsible for regulating our physiological functions and emotions. When we are under stress or pressure, our unconscious mind can cause us to react in a way that is not aligned with our conscious goals and values. For example, a leader who is under stress may become irritable, aggressive, or dismissive, which can negatively impact their relationships with others and their ability to lead effectively.

The conscious, subconscious, and unconscious mind are all interrelated and play a role in shaping our leadership style and behaviour. Understanding the influence of each of these components on our leadership can help us identify and address unconscious biases and beliefs that may be limiting our effectiveness as leaders. Additionally, developing self-awareness and mindfulness can help us become more conscious of our thoughts, emotions, and behaviours and cause us to make more intentional and effective leadership decisions.

The development of conscious, subconscious, and unconscious aspects of leadership plays a critical role in the success of a leader. Understanding these aspects of the psyche can help a leader develop the skills and habits necessary for effective leadership.

Conscious leadership refers to the intentional and deliberate actions a leader takes to achieve a desired outcome. This includes a leader's ability to make decisions, communicate effectively, and motivate their team. Conscious leadership requires a deeper understanding of one's values, strengths, and weaknesses, as well as a strong sense of self-awareness.

Subconscious leadership refers to the underlying thought patterns and behaviours that are formed from a person's experiences and conditioning. This includes biases, habits, and emotional responses that are often unconscious. Subconscious leadership can either support or hinder conscious leadership efforts.

Unconscious leadership refers to the deeper aspects of the psyche that are not easily accessible to our conscious awareness. This includes the deep-seated beliefs, values, and emotions that shape a person's leadership style and behaviour. Understanding the unconscious aspects of leadership can help a leader identify and overcome limiting beliefs and behaviours, leading to greater self-awareness and personal growth.

To develop conscious, subconscious, and unconscious aspects of leadership, a leader can employ a variety of strategies and tools, including:

Mindfulness and self-reflection: By taking time to reflect on their thoughts, feelings, and behaviours, a leader can gain a greater insight into their conscious and subconscious aspects of leadership.

Coaching and mentorship: Working with a coach or mentor can help a leader identify and overcome limiting beliefs and behaviours and develop the skills and habits necessary for effective leadership.

Neuro-linguistic programming (NLP) and other psycho-therapeutic techniques: These techniques can help a leader identify and overcome limiting beliefs and behaviours and develop greater self-awareness and personal growth.

Emotional intelligence training: Emotional intelligence training can help a leader develop the skills and habits necessary for effective leadership. **Journaling and goal setting:** Writing down goals and tracking progress can help a leader stay focused and motivated and develop the skills and habits necessary for effective leadership.

By developing the conscious, subconscious, and unconscious aspects of leadership, a leader can become more effective, resilient, and adaptable. This can lead to improved relationships with others, greater personal and professional growth, and, ultimately, more impactful and fulfilling leadership.

Leadership is a vital aspect of modern society that requires individuals to have the ability to influence, inspire and motivate others. One key aspect of leadership that often goes overlooked is the impact that conscious, subconscious, and unconscious thought patterns can have on a leader's ability to influence and inspire those around them.

Conscious thought patterns are thoughts that are deliberately and actively directed by a person. These thoughts are the product of conscious decision-making and conscious intention. A leader who is aware of their conscious thought patterns has the ability to control their thoughts and emotions, which can be a valuable tool in controlling the influence they have over others.

Subconscious thought patterns are thought patterns that are automatic and often operate outside of our conscious awareness. These thoughts are the result of habits and patterns of behaviour that have been formed over time. A leader who is aware of their subconscious thought patterns and habits can work to modify and change these patterns in order to improve their ability to influence and inspire others.

Unconscious thought patterns are thoughts that are outside a person's control and awareness. These thoughts are driven by deeply ingrained beliefs, values, and emotions that often shape a person's behaviour and decision-making skills. A leader who is aware of their unconscious thought patterns can work to identify and modify these thoughts in order to improve their ability to influence and inspire others.

The process of developing conscious, subconscious, and unconscious thought patterns as part of a leadership development program requires a multi-step approach. The first step is to become aware of the thoughts, beliefs, and values that are driving your behaviour. This can be done through self-reflection, therapy, or through the use of psychometric assessments.

The second step is to modify the thought patterns that are hindering your ability to be an effective leader. This can be done through techniques such as cognitive-behavioural therapy, mindfulness, and positive affirmations.

Leaders can improve upon their ability to control their influence by actively working to change their conscious, subconscious, and unconscious thought patterns. This can be done through intentional and deliberate thought, self-reflection, and continuous improvement.

Developing conscious, subconscious, and unconscious thought patterns is an important aspect of leadership development. By becoming aware of their thoughts, beliefs, and values, leaders can improve their ability to influence and inspire others. Through a multi-step approach that includes self-reflection, therapy, and intentional change, leaders can achieve greater levels of influence and effectiveness in their leadership roles.

In order to effectively lead, they must understand and navigate through the interplay between their conscious, subconscious, and unconscious minds. However, there are certain pitfalls that leaders must avoid in order to ensure that their influence is positive and productive.

First and foremost, leaders should avoid unconsciously projecting their own biases and prejudices onto their team members and decision-making processes. This can lead to discrimination and an unwelcoming workplace culture, which can have negative impacts on employee morale and productivity. To combat this, leaders must be mindful of their unconscious thoughts and beliefs and actively work to counteract any biases that may affect their leadership style.

Another trap leaders must avoid is allowing their subconscious to control their actions without reflection. Leaders may have deeply ingrained habits and tendencies that can negatively impact their decision-making, such as a tendency to make hasty decisions without fully considering all options. To address this, leaders must take their time to reflect on their thought processes and understand how their subconscious mind is influencing their actions.

Leaders must also be aware of their unconscious habits and tendencies when it comes to communication. For example, they may have an unconscious habit of interrupting others, which can make team members feel disrespected and undermine their confidence. Leaders must actively work to recognise and address these unconscious and negative communication habits in order to build strong, collaborative relationships with their teams.

Leaders should avoid becoming overly reliant on their conscious mind while neglecting their subconscious and unconscious. Leaders who rely too heavily on their conscious thoughts may miss out on important insights and intuition that can inform their decision-making and improve their leadership abilities. Instead, leaders should strive to balance their conscious and unconscious thought processes in order to make informed and well-rounded decisions.

Leaders must be mindful of the interplay between their conscious, subconscious, and unconscious mind in order to avoid negative influences and cause them to become effective leaders. By avoiding unconscious biases, reflecting on subconscious tendencies, and balancing conscious and unconscious thought processes, leaders can cultivate a leadership style that is both effective and inclusive.

PART-34

LEADERSHIP VS AUTOMATION AND ARTIFICIAL INTELLIGENCE (AI)

In today's rapidly advancing technology landscape, the role of managers and automation has become a hotly debated topic. Some believe that automation and artificial intelligence will eventually replace managers and human leadership, while others argue that managers and leaders will always be necessary to provide guidance and direction in a rapidly changing world.

From a technological perspective, automation has become increasingly sophisticated and can perform many tasks that were previously only possible for humans to do. Automation can complete routine tasks, improve efficiency, and reduce the cost of labour. However, the reality is that technology is still far from being able to fully replicate human decision-making and problem-solving skills, especially in complex and rapidly changing environments.

In these situations, managers and leaders play a crucial role in guiding and directing employees, providing decision-making support, and making critical decisions that shape the organisation's future. Managers and leaders are also responsible for developing and nurturing a workplace culture that is inclusive and values collaboration, creativity, and innovation. They must be able to anticipate and respond to changes in the business environment and lead their teams through the challenges and opportunities that arise.

Leadership is also important in managing the transition to automation, as they must help employees understand and adapt to new technology and provide support and training to help employees develop the skills they need to work effectively with automation. Leaders must also be prepared to handle any negative impacts that automation may have on employees, such as job loss or reduced job security.

In conclusion, the role of managers and leaders in an era of automation is to balance the benefits of technology with the importance of human skills and relationships. Managers and leaders must be able to effectively use technology to achieve their goals while also developing and nurturing the human skills that are essential for success in a rapidly changing world. They must be able to lead their organisations through change and help employees adapt to new technology and new ways of working.

One of the main risks posed by automation to managers is the risk of job loss. With automation taking over many manual tasks, managers are facing the threat of becoming redundant. Automation has the ability to perform tasks faster, more efficiently, and with fewer errors, which can result in job loss for managers. This can be a major concern for managers who have been working with a company for a long time and are now facing the risk of losing their livelihood.

Another risk associated with automation is the loss of control. Managers have traditionally been responsible for overseeing a team of employees and ensuring that tasks are completed on time and done to the required standards. However, with automation, many of these tasks are now being performed by machines, which can make managers feel like they are losing control over their working environment. This can be particularly challenging for managers who are used to having a significant level of control and autonomy over their working environment.

Additionally, automation can also lead to a loss of skills and knowledge on the part of managers. Managers who have been working in a particular industry for a long time have built up a wealth of experience and knowledge. However, with automation, many of these skills and knowledge may become obsolete, which can make managers feel like their careers are no longer relevant. This can lead to a lack of motivation and a decline in job satisfaction.

To mitigate these risks, managers need to adapt and evolve their skillset to keep pace with automation. They can do this by staying up-to-date with the latest technology and trends and by developing new skills that are in demand. For example, managers can focus on developing their leadership and communication skills, as these skills will always be in demand, regardless of the level of automation.

The risk of automation to managers is real and significant, but it is not insurmountable. By adapting and evolving their skillset, managers can mitigate the risks posed by automation and continue to play a vital role in the workplace. Leadership will play a crucial role in helping managers to make this transition by providing support, guidance, and training to help them develop the skills and knowledge they need to thrive in the age of automation.

The advancement of technology has greatly impacted the world of work, and the rise of automation and artificial intelligence (AI) has changed the landscape of many industries. The integration of these technologies in the workplace has brought about many benefits, but it also poses a challenge for managers. The shift from manual tasks to automation and AI can result in managers feeling less relevant, leading to decreased morale and motivation. As a leader, it is important to understand and manage the impact of automation on managers to minimise any negative effects and ensure their continued success.

One of the key ways to minimise the negative effects of automation on managers is by investing in their professional development. This includes providing training and upskilling opportunities that can help managers adapt to the changing work environment. Leaders can provide opportunities for managers to learn new skills and improve their knowledge of automation and AI, thereby making them more confident and competent in their roles. This will help managers feel more empowered and capable of leveraging technology to achieve better results.

Another way to minimise the impact of automation on managers is by involving them in the planning and implementation process. By involving managers in the decision-making process, leaders can ensure that their manager's opinions and concerns are taken into account. This can also help managers feel more connected to the process and more invested in the outcome. Moreover, it can also give them a sense of ownership over the technology, leading to a more positive attitude toward automation.

Leaders can also support managers by providing them with the resources and tools they need to leverage technology effectively. This includes providing access to technology, training on its use, and support when needed. This will help managers feel more confident in their ability to use technology and better understand how it can improve their work.

Finally, leaders can also support managers by creating a positive work culture that values human interaction and collaboration. Automation and AI can result in a more isolated working environment, but leaders can help to counteract this by promoting team-building activities and fostering a positive workplace culture. By emphasizing the importance of human interaction, leaders can help managers feel more connected and engaged in their work, even in an automated environment.

The integration of automation and AI in the workplace can pose a challenge for managers, but leaders have a critical role to play in minimizing the negative impact of these technologies. By investing in professional development, involving managers in the planning process, providing resources and support, and promoting a positive work culture, leaders can ensure that managers remain engaged and motivated in their roles.

One of the key reasons managers may lose their jobs to automation is because of their lack of human touch in certain tasks. Automated systems are designed to perform specific tasks more efficiently and with fewer errors than human workers. However, these systems lack the emotional intelligence and empathy that human workers possess, which can be important in customer-facing roles and building relationships with clients. When tasks such as customer service and relationship management are automated, managers who specialise in these areas may find themselves out of work.

Another factor that may contribute to the loss of jobs for managers is the limited ability of automation to handle complex and unstructured tasks. Despite the advancements in AI technology, automated systems are still not sophisticated enough to handle complex decision-making processes or tasks that require creativity and problem-solving skills. As a result, managers who specialise in these areas may also find themselves at risk of losing their jobs to automation.

Finally, the speed at which automation and AI are being integrated into businesses is also a concern for managers. Many managers may not have the skills or training required to adapt to the new technological landscape and may find it difficult to compete with automation for job opportunities. This can be particularly challenging for managers who are not familiar with technology and are not comfortable working in a technology-driven environment.

Leadership plays a crucial role in mitigating the negative effects of automation on managers. Leaders must therefore ensure that managers are equipped with the skills and training necessary to adapt to the changing technological landscape. This may involve providing training in new technologies and tools, as well as offering support and guidance as managers navigate through the transition. Additionally, leaders must ensure that managers are not left behind in the race for job opportunities and that they are provided with the resources and support they need to remain competitive in the job market.

In conclusion, the integration of automation and AI into the workplace has the potential to bring about many benefits, but it also poses significant risks to managers. Leaders must take steps to mitigate these risks by providing training and support to managers and ensuring that they are not left behind in the race for job opportunities. By doing so, leaders can help managers adapt to the changing technological landscape and thereby minimise the negative effects of automation on their careers.

Leadership is crucial in fostering a culture of innovation and creativity, as they provide the vision and direction that drives the organisation forward. With the advent of automation and AI, leaders must find new and creative ways to utilise technology to enhance their operations. By leveraging these tools, leaders can optimise their processes, increase efficiency, and provide better services to their customers. However, leaders must be mindful of the fact that automation and AI can only do so much and that human creativity and innovation remain critical components of any successful organisation.

Leaders can encourage creativity and innovation by providing a supportive and inclusive working environment that values new ideas and encourages risk-taking. Leaders can also invest in training and development programs that help employees develop the skills and knowledge necessary to embrace new technologies and generate innovative ideas. Additionally, leaders can promote collaboration and encourage employees to work together to find new solutions to problems.

Leaders must also understand that innovation and creativity cannot be automated. While AI and automation can assist in streamlining operations and improving efficiency, they cannot replace the human touch that is essential for true innovation and creativity. Leaders must therefore find ways to balance the use of technology with the need for human interaction and creativity.

Leaders play a critical role in fostering innovation and creativity in the era of automation and AI. By creating a working environment that values and encourages new ideas, investing in employee development, promoting collaboration, and balancing the use of technology with human interaction, leaders can ensure their organisations remain competitive and relevant in the rapidly changing landscape of business.

PART-35

IQ AND INTELLIGENCE OF LEADERSHIP

Intelligence quotient (IQ) has long been considered a measure of one's mental ability or potential. While IQ tests were once seen as the ultimate measure of intelligence, they have since been widely criticised for not accurately capturing the complexity of human intelligence and its various components. The concept of intelligence and its relationship to leadership is more complex than what a single test score can tell us.

Leadership, like intelligence, is a complex phenomenon that can be influenced by various factors, including emotional intelligence, experience, education, and cultural background. While intelligence can certainly be a valuable asset for leaders, it is not the only determining factor for success in leadership roles. In fact, emotional intelligence has been found to be more predictive of success in leadership positions than IQ.

Leaders with higher emotional intelligence are better equipped to navigate through complex social and interpersonal relationships, understand the motivations of their team members, and respond to their needs effectively. They are also able to recognise their own strengths and weaknesses, work through conflicts and challenges, and adapt to changing circumstances. In contrast, leaders with high IQ but low emotional intelligence may struggle to effectively lead and inspire their teams and may be perceived as cold, distant, and unapproachable.

Furthermore, it's important to remember that IQ is only one aspect of a person's overall intelligence and can be influenced by a range of external factors, such as environment and upbringing. IQ may not necessarily reflect their innate abilities or leadership potential. In this sense, IQ should be considered one factor among many when evaluating the potential for leadership.

In conclusion, the relationship between IQ and intelligence in the context of leadership is complex and nuanced. While IQ can certainly be an indicator of intellectual ability, it is not the only factor that determines success in leadership roles. Emotional intelligence, experience, education, and cultural background all play a critical role in shaping a person's leadership potential. Ultimately, the most successful leaders are those who possess a combination of intellectual, emotional, and interpersonal intelligence that allows them to effectively lead and inspire their teams.

Intelligence Quotient (IQ) and intelligence have long been considered important indicators of a person's potential to be a successful leader. However, while IQ and intelligence are important components of an individual's ability to lead, they are by no means the only factors that determine a person's leadership potential. In fact, relying solely on IQ and intelligence scores as the primary criteria for leadership selection can be detrimental to the development of effective leadership within an organisation.

One of the primary problems with using IQ and intelligence as the sole criteria for leadership selection is that they only measure a person's cognitive abilities and do not take into account the individual's emotional intelligence or social skills. Emotional intelligence is considered by many to be a critical component of effective leadership. Social skills, on the other hand, refer to a person's ability to communicate, collaborate, and build relationships with others. Both emotional intelligence and social skills are crucial for leaders to be able to influence and engage their followers and lead a team toward a common goal.

Another problem with using IQ and intelligence as the sole criteria for leadership selection is that they do not account for an individual's personal values, beliefs, and motivations. These are important factors that shape a person's leadership style and impact how they approach decision-making and problem-solving. For example, an individual who values integrity and honesty may approach decision-making differently than someone who values power and control. A leader's personal values, beliefs, and motivations play a significant role in how they lead; thus, ignoring these factors can result in ineffective leadership.

Finally, relying solely on IQ and intelligence scores can limit the diversity of perspectives and approaches within an organisation. This can lead to a homogeneous leadership culture that is not capable of adapting to changing circumstances and may miss opportunities for innovation and growth. An organisation with a diverse leadership team, on the other hand, can benefit from a wider range of perspectives and approaches, allowing it to be more agile and responsive to change.

While IQ and intelligence are important components of an individual's ability to lead, they should not be the sole criteria for leadership selection. An effective leader requires a combination of cognitive abilities, emotional intelligence, social skills, personal values, beliefs, and motivations, as well as a willingness to continuously learn and grow. Organisations should consider these factors when evaluating leadership potential and strive to build a diverse leadership team that reflects the values, beliefs, and motivations of the organisation.

Intelligence and IQ are two important factors that can contribute to the development of leadership skills. However, it is important to understand that these are not the only determinants of leadership. While IQ and intelligence are important, they are not the only qualities that make a great leader. Other qualities such as emotional intelligence, communication skills, empathy, and adaptability also play a crucial role in developing leadership skills.

To develop IQ and intelligence in the context of leadership, there are several steps that one can follow.

Firstly, it is important to engage in continuous learning and self-development. This can be achieved by reading books, attending workshops, and taking courses that are relevant to your field. Additionally, it is important to seek out mentorship and coaching from individuals who have experience and expertise in your field.

Another important step in developing IQ and intelligence is to cultivate critical thinking skills. This means that you need to be able to analyse and evaluate information and situations and come up with creative solutions to problems. This requires an open mind and the ability to question assumptions and conventional wisdom.

It is also important to develop a growth mindset. This means that you should approach challenges and setbacks as opportunities for growth rather than seeing them as obstacles. By embracing a growth mindset, you will be more likely to learn from your experiences and develop your skills and knowledge over time.

Finally, developing a strong network and seeking out opportunities for collaboration can also help to enhance IQ and intelligence in the context of leadership. Collaborating with others allows you to learn from their perspectives, expand your own knowledge, and develop new skills. By working with others, you can also develop your ability to communicate effectively, solve problems collectively, and lead a team toward a common goal.

Developing IQ and intelligence in the context of leadership is a continuous process that requires effort and dedication. However, by engaging in continuous learning, cultivating critical thinking skills, embracing a growth mindset, and seeking out opportunities for collaboration, you can develop these important qualities and become a more effective leader.

PART-36

THE "HOW" AND "WHY" IN LEADERSHIP

The "how" and "why" concepts in leadership refer to the means and the purpose of leadership, respectively. The "how" refers to the strategies, processes, and tactics that a leader employs to achieve their objectives. This could include things like communication style, delegation, and decision-making. On the other hand, the "why" refers to the leader's motivation and purpose for leading. This includes the values, beliefs, and goals that drive their actions. The relationship between the "how" and "why" in leadership is essential for leaders to be effective. Leaders who only focus on the "how" without understanding the "why" may find it difficult to gain the support and commitment of their followers. On the other hand, leaders who only focus on the "why" without considering the "how" may struggle to translate their vision into action.

Leaders need to be able to balance the "how" and "why" concepts in order to be successful. A leader who has a clear understanding of their "why" and can communicate it effectively can inspire and motivate their followers. This can result in increased engagement, commitment, and accountability from their followers, which can ultimately lead to better outcomes.

However, the "how" is just as important as the "why". A leader must have a solid understanding of the practical steps and processes needed to achieve their goals. They must have the skills and knowledge to effectively implement their plans and overcome obstacles.

In conclusion, the relationship between the "how" and "why" in leadership is complex and interdependent. Leaders must be able to effectively balance the two in order to be successful and achieve their goals. A leader who can effectively communicate their "why" while also having the practical skills and knowledge to implement their plans will be able to inspire and motivate their followers and ultimately achieve better outcomes.

To develop the "how" and "why" in leadership, leaders need to go through a step-by-step process to gain a better understanding of their own leadership style and their motivations for leadership. Here are the steps to develop the "how" and "why" in leadership:

Self-reflection: This is the first and most important step in developing the "how" and "why" in leadership. Leaders need to take their time to reflect on their own leadership style, their motivations, and their strengths and weaknesses. They should ask themselves questions such as: What drives me to lead? What are my strengths and weaknesses as a leader? What are my leadership goals?

Seek feedback: Leaders should seek feedback from their team members, colleagues, and mentors to gain a better understanding of their leadership style and what areas they need to work on. This feedback can be in the form of regular performance evaluations, informal conversations, or 360-degree feedback assessments.

Study leadership: Leaders should invest time and effort into studying leadership. They can do this by reading books, attending workshops, and taking courses on leadership. Leaders should also study the leadership styles of successful leaders and seek to understand what makes them successful leaders.

Practice: Leaders should put into practice the methods and techniques they learn through their studies and feedback. This could involve experimenting with new approaches to leadership, such as delegating more responsibilities, engaging in active listening, or encouraging teamwork.

Continuous improvement: Leaders should continuously assess their progress and seek to improve their leadership skills. They should regularly seek feedback from colleagues or mentors and seek to understand their impact on their team and their organisation.

Developing the "how" and "why" in leadership is a continuous process that requires self-reflection, feedback, study, practice, and continuous improvement. By following these steps, leaders can gain a better understanding of their own leadership style and motivations and become effective in leading their teams and organisations to success.

For instance, let's consider a leader in a technological company who is tasked with implementing a new project that involves a major shift in the company's operations. To develop the "how" and "why" in this scenario, the leader would need to take the following steps:

Step 1: Understanding the "Why"

The first step in developing the "how" and "why" in leadership is to understand the "why" behind the project. In this case, the leader should start by identifying the reasons for the shift in operations, such as staying competitive in the market, improving efficiency, or adapting to changes in the industry. Understanding the "why" of the project is essential because it provides a clear vision and purpose for the team, which is necessary for successful implementation.

Step 2: Developing the "How"

Once the "why" has been identified, the next step is to develop the "how". In this scenario, the leader should start by conducting a comprehensive analysis of the current operations and identifying the best ways to achieve the desired shift. This could involve exploring new technologies, processes, or systems that can help improve efficiency and competitiveness. The leader should also engage with their team members and other stakeholders to get their perspectives and insights.

Step 3: Communicating the "How" and "Why"

Once the "how" has been developed, it's important to communicate it effectively to the team and other stakeholders. The leader should clearly explain the reasons for the shift in operations and how it will help the company better achieve its goals. They should also explain how the team and other stakeholders will be involved in the implementation process and what their roles and responsibilities will be.

Step 4: Empowering the Team

The next step is to empower the team to carry out the implementation of the project. This could involve providing training, resources, and support to help them perform their tasks effectively. The leader should also provide opportunities for feedback and continuous improvement, encourage the team to take ownership of the project, and contribute their ideas and insights.

Step 5: Monitoring Progress

Finally, the leader should monitor progress and make adjustments as and when needed. This could involve regularly checking in with the team, tracking key metrics, and making changes to the implementation plan based on feedback and performance data.

The development of "how" and "why" in leadership involves a systematic and collaborative approach that starts with understanding the "why" behind a project or initiative, developing the "how" through analysis and engagement, communicating the "how" and "why" effectively to team members, empowering the team, and monitoring progress. This approach helps leaders align their teams around a shared vision and purpose and ensures that everyone is working towards the same goals.

PART-37

TEAM EMPOWERMENT

Team empowerment is a crucial aspect of effective leadership. It refers to the process of granting decision-making authority and control to team members, with the goal of increasing motivation, job satisfaction, and productivity. When team members feel empowered, they are more likely to take ownership of their work, be more engaged and committed to the success of the team, and develop a greater sense of purpose and meaning in their work.

Leaders play a critical role in the process of team empowerment. They must create the conditions that enable team members to take on more responsibility and be more involved in decision-making. This requires leaders to be clear about the goals and objectives of the team, communicate these goals effectively to team members, and establish a supportive culture that fosters innovation and creativity. Leaders must also provide the necessary resources and support that enable team members to do their work effectively and recognise and reward their efforts and achievements.

One key aspect of team empowerment is delegation. Leaders must be able to delegate tasks and responsibilities to team members and trust them to carry out these tasks effectively. This requires leaders to have a clearer understanding of the strengths and weaknesses of each team member and assign tasks and responsibilities accordingly. Leaders must also be willing to share control and provide team members with the necessary resources and support to succeed.

Another key aspect of team empowerment is communication. Leaders must be able to communicate effectively with team members, listen to their ideas and feedback, and involve them in decision-making processes. This requires leaders to have strong interpersonal skills, be approachable and accessible, and be able to build trust and rapport with team members. Leaders must also be able to communicate the goals and objectives of the team in a way that inspires and motivates team members.

Finally, team empowerment requires leaders to be able to provide feedback and coaching to team members. This requires leaders to have a deeper understanding of the development needs of each team member and to be able to provide constructive feedback that helps them grow and improve. Leaders must also be able to recognise and reward the efforts and achievements of team members and provide them with opportunities for growth and development.

Team empowerment is a critical aspect of effective leadership. It requires leaders to create the conditions that enable team members to take on more responsibility, be more involved in decision-making, and be more engaged and committed to the success of the team. Leaders must also provide the necessary resources and support, delegate tasks and responsibilities effectively, communicate effectively with team members, and provide feedback and coaching that helps team members grow and improve. By doing so, leaders can create high-performing teams that are able to achieve great results and make a meaningful impact on the organisations they serve.

Empowerment has several types and levels, and leaders can implement different approaches to empower their teams based on their goals, the type of work they do, and the team's capabilities. In this essay, we will explore the different types and levels of team empowerment in leadership:

Delegation of Authority: This type of empowerment involves assigning specific tasks and responsibilities to team members and granting them the authority to make decisions related to those tasks. This approach helps leaders to reduce their workload, increase the speed of decision-making, and enhance the creativity and innovation of the team. Leaders can delegate authority based on the skills and experience of their team members, which creates a sense of ownership and responsibility in the team.

Sharing of Information: Sharing information with the team is another form of empowerment, which enables them to understand the organisation's goals and objectives, as well as the context of their work. By providing team members with the necessary information, leaders can increase their trust, engagement, and motivation. It also helps leaders to make better decisions and foster a more open and transparent culture.

Decision Making: Encouraging team members to participate in decision-making processes is another type of empowerment. This type of empowerment requires leaders to trust their team and delegate the decision-making power to them, which enhances their sense of ownership and responsibility.

Team members are more likely to be motivated and engaged when they have a voice and feel like they are contributing to the success of the team.

Empowerment through Skills Development: Developing the skills and abilities of team members is another way of empowering them. Leaders can invest in training programs, workshops, and other learning opportunities that help team members grow and improve their skills. This type of empowerment leads to increased confidence, motivation, and engagement, as well as improved performance and productivity.

Levels of Empowerment: Empowerment can also be categorised based on the level of authority and responsibility delegated to team members. Low-level empowerment might involve delegating routine tasks or providing information, while high-level empowerment might involve delegating decision-making power or empowering team members to develop their skills. Leaders can determine the level of empowerment based on the stage of their team's development, the complexity of the work they do, and the level of trust they have in their team members.

Team empowerment refers to the process of giving team members the autonomy, resources, and support to make decisions, take ownership of their work, and drive results. Empowered teams have a greater sense of ownership and commitment to their work, which results in higher engagement, productivity, and creativity. In this essay, we will discuss the step-by-step process of empowering a team in the context of leadership.

Step 1: Define Goals and Objectives

The first step in empowering a team is to define clear goals and objectives. This involves working with the team to identify what they want to achieve and what they need to do to reach their goals. Defining goals and objectives helps to create a shared understanding of what the team is working towards, which is essential for team empowerment.

Step 2: Assign Responsibilities and Accountabilities

The next step is to assign responsibilities and accountabilities to team members. This involves clarifying who is responsible for what and ensuring that each team member has a clear understanding of their role and what they are accountable for. This helps to ensure that the team is working towards a common goal and that everyone knows what they are responsible for.

Step 3: Provide Resources and Support

Team empowerment requires that team members have access to the resources and support they need to do their job effectively. This includes access to tools, training, and development opportunities. Leaders need to be proactive in identifying what resources and support their team needs and ensuring that they have access to these resources.

Step 4: Encourage Collaboration and Communication

Effective communication and collaboration are critical components of team empowerment. Leaders need to create an environment where team members feel comfortable sharing their ideas, opinions, and feedback. This can involve regular team meetings, open communication channels, and opportunities for team members to collaborate on projects and initiatives.

Step 5: Foster a Culture of Trust and Respect

A culture of trust and respect is essential for team empowerment. Leaders need to establish trust by being transparent, honest, and reliable. They also need to foster a culture of respect by encouraging open and honest communication, recognizing and valuing the contributions of team members, and treating everyone with dignity and respect.

Step 6: Provide Opportunities for Growth and Development

Finally, leaders need to provide opportunities for growth and development to empower their team members. This can include training and development programs, mentorship opportunities, and opportunities to take on new challenges and responsibilities. Providing opportunities for growth and development helps to build the skills and competencies of team members and enables them to take on new challenges with confidence.

Team empowerment is a crucial aspect of leadership that involves giving team members the autonomy, resources, and support to make decisions, take ownership of their work, and drive results in their organisation. The step-by-step process of team empowerment involves defining goals and objectives, assigning responsibilities and accountabilities, providing resources and support, encouraging collaboration and communication, fostering a culture of trust and respect, and providing opportunities for growth and development. By empowering their teams, leaders can create a more engaged, productive, and creative workforce that is better equipped to achieve their goals and objectives.

PART-38

THE FUTURE OF LEADERSHIP

The future of leadership is a topic of much discussion and speculation as the world continues to evolve and change at an unprecedented pace. While it is impossible to predict the future with certainty, there are several trends and factors that are likely going to shape the future of leadership.

One of the biggest trends that will impact the future of leadership is the increasing importance of technology. As technology continues to advance, leaders will need to be able to understand and use it effectively in order to stay competitive. This will require a deeper understanding of digital tools and platforms, as well as the ability to leverage these tools to achieve business goals.

Another trend that is likely to impact the future of leadership is the increasing importance of diversity and inclusiveness. As the global population becomes increasingly diverse, leaders will need to be able to work effectively with people from a variety of backgrounds, cultures, and perspectives. This will require a deeper understanding of different cultures and a commitment to creating inclusive environments where everyone can thrive.

In addition, the future of leadership is likely to be shaped by the changing nature of work and the workforce. The rise of the gig economy and the increasing prevalence of remote work are likely to challenge traditional leadership models, and this will require leaders to adopt new approaches.

Despite these challenges, the future of leadership is also likely to be shaped by positive trends and opportunities. For example, the growing importance of sustainability and environmental responsibility is likely to create new opportunities for leaders to drive positive change and make a positive impact in the world.

The financial impact of these trends is difficult to predict, but it is likely that companies that invest in developing their leaders and preparing them for the future will be more successful than those that do not. Companies that are able to stay ahead of the curve in terms of technology and diversity will be better positioned to compete in the global marketplace and achieve their business goals.

The future of leadership is likely to be shaped by a variety of trends and factors, including technology, diversity, the changing nature of work, and sustainability. While there are certainly challenges that leaders will need to overcome, there are also opportunities for growth and impact. Companies that invest in developing their leaders and preparing them for the future are likely to be the most successful.

The technology industry is one of the fastest-growing and most dynamic industries of the 21st century. With the rise of digital transformation and the increasing reliance on technology in our daily lives, the role of leadership in the tech industry has never been more important. In this section, we will explore the future of leadership in the tech industry, including the challenges and opportunities that lie ahead and the impact of technology on the way leaders will lead in the future.

The first challenge that leaders in the tech industry face is the rapid pace of change. Technology is constantly evolving, and the tech industry is no exception. The ability to keep up with these changes and respond to them effectively will be critical to the success of tech industry leaders. In order to do this, leaders will need to be flexible, agile, and proactive, constantly seeking out new opportunities and adapting their strategies to meet the changing needs of the market.

Another challenge facing tech industry leaders is the increasing competition for talent. As the demand for technology continues to grow, so does the competition for the best and brightest minds in the industry. Leaders will need to be innovative in their approach to attracting, retaining, and developing the talent they need to succeed. This will require a deeper understanding of the skills and capabilities that their teams possess and the ability to match these with the changing needs of the business.

The rise of technology also presents opportunities for tech industry leaders. One of the biggest opportunities is the ability to leverage technology to gain a competitive advantage. For example, the use of data analytics and artificial intelligence can help leaders make more informed decisions, improve their operations and drive innovation. In addition, the use of digital platforms and social media can help leaders connect with their customers, stakeholders, and employees in new and more meaningful ways.

Another opportunity is the ability to create new business models and revenue streams. With the rise of the Internet of Things (IoT) and the increasing use of connected devices, there is a growing opportunity for tech industry leaders to create new products and services that can help solve problems and meet the needs of their customers in new and innovative ways.

The impact of technology on the future of leadership in the tech industry is also likely to be significant. For example, the increasing use of automation and AI is likely to change the way that leaders lead, requiring them to be more strategic and less operational in their approach. In addition, the use of virtual and augmented reality is likely to change the way that leaders communicate and collaborate with their teams, allowing them to create more immersive and interactive experiences.

The future of leadership in the tech industry is likely to be shaped by the challenges and opportunities presented by technology. Leaders will need to be flexible, innovative, and proactive, constantly seeking out new opportunities and adapting their strategies to meet the changing needs of the market. They will also need to be strategic, leveraging technology to gain a competitive advantage and create new business models and revenue streams. With the right approach, the future of leadership in the tech industry is likely to be bright, offering a wealth of opportunities for those who are prepared to seize them.

Leadership is a critical component in any organisation, including the tech and entrepreneurship space. It is a driving force that can shape the direction and success of any company. In the tech and entrepreneurship space, the leadership landscape is rapidly evolving, with new technologies and business models emerging every day. As a result, leaders must adapt to these changes and continually develop their skills to remain effective.

The tech and entrepreneurship space is characterised by innovation, risk-taking, and agility. To succeed in this environment, leaders must possess a unique combination of technical expertise, creative vision, and the ability to inspire and motivate others. They must be able to make quick decisions, adapt to change, and remain focused on the big picture while managing the day-to-day operations of their organisations.

One of the most important qualities that leaders in the tech and entrepreneurship space must possess is the ability to embrace technology. They must be able to understand and utilise the latest technologies to drive their organisations forward. This includes not only understanding the technical aspects of these tools but also being able to utilise them to increase efficiency, improve customer experience, and achieve business goals.

Another critical quality is the ability to foster a culture of innovation and creativity. Leaders in the tech and entrepreneurship space must create a working environment where employees are encouraged to take risks, experiment, and bring their ideas to the table. This culture of innovation and creativity is essential for staying ahead in a constantly evolving marketplace.

Financial impact is another important aspect of leadership in the tech and entrepreneurship space. Leaders must be able to effectively manage their organisation's finances and make sound investments in technology, infrastructure, and personnel. They must also be able to balance short-term financial goals with their long-term strategic vision.

The future of leadership in the tech and entrepreneurship space is uncertain, but it is likely to be shaped by technological advancements and changes in consumer behaviour. As new technologies emerge, leaders will need to continually improve their skills and strategies to stay ahead of the curve. For example, the rise of artificial intelligence and machine learning is likely to have a significant impact on the way organisations operate, and leaders will need to be prepared to leverage these technologies to improve their operations and better serve their customers.

The leadership landscape in the tech and entrepreneurship space is rapidly evolving, and leaders must possess a unique combination of technical expertise, creative vision, and the ability to inspire and motivate others. They must also be able to embrace technology, foster a culture of innovation and creativity, and effectively manage their organisation's finances. The future of leadership in this space is uncertain, but leaders must be prepared to adapt to change and stay ahead of the curve.

SUMMARY

The impact of coaching on leadership can be significant, as it provides leaders with a space to reflect on their practices and learn new skills. Studies have shown that coaching can lead to improved job satisfaction, increased productivity, and better leadership performance.

The psychology behind leadership is a complex field that encompasses various factors such as emotional intelligence, cognitive biases, and personality traits. Leaders who understand their own psychology and the psychology of their team can be more effective in managing conflicts, communicating their vision, and inspiring their followers.

The future of leadership in the tech industry is rapidly evolving as technology is transforming the way we work and live. Leaders in the tech industry must embrace innovation, adapt to change, and be able to navigate through the complexities of the digital landscape.

Agility in leadership refers to the ability of leaders to adapt to changing circumstances, respond to unexpected challenges, and pivot their strategies when necessary. Developing agility in leadership requires a growth mindset, a willingness to experiment, and an ability to embrace failure as a learning opportunity.

Innovative leaders are those who are able to think outside the box, challenge the status quo, and bring new ideas and solutions to the table. Innovative leaders often possess traits such as creativity, curiosity, and a willingness to take risks.

Habit change is a critical component of leadership development, as it helps leaders cultivate new skills and behaviours. The 66-day habit change model is a popular approach, which suggests that it takes approximately 66 days to form a new habit. Leaders can also benefit from shock adaptation, where a significant change or disruption forces them to break out from their old patterns and embrace new behaviours.

Barber leadership can also provide valuable insights into leadership skills and behaviours, as barbers often have to navigate through complex interpersonal relationships and provide their customers with high-quality experiences. Leaders can learn from barbers by developing their interpersonal skills, paying close attention to detail, and providing their followers with a sense of comfort and trust.

Psychometric assessments and tools can be useful in determining traditional traits of leadership, such as emotional intelligence, cognitive biases, and personality traits. However, it is important to understand that these assessments are not perfect science and may not always accurately reflect a leader's capabilities.

The interplay of the conscious, subconscious, and unconscious mind can have a significant impact on leadership. Leaders who are aware of their conscious, subconscious, and unconscious biases and tendencies can work to overcome them and improve their leadership abilities. Leaders can also develop their conscious, subconscious, and unconscious mind through self-reflection, mindfulness, and ongoing learning.

In conclusion, leadership is a complex and multi-faceted field that encompasses various skills, traits, and habits. Understanding the impact of coaching, the psychology behind leadership, the future of leadership, agility in leadership, innovative leaders, habit change, barber leadership, psychometric assessments, and the interplay of the conscious, subconscious, and unconscious mind can help leaders become more effective and impactful in their roles.

Leadership is a complex and multi-faceted concept that encompasses a wide range of habits, skills, and results. It is an earned description of collective outcomes achieved through time and effort spent developing the necessary traits and characteristics. While many people may be skilled at performing their job, true leadership goes beyond job performance and requires the ability to influence and humanise others.

Leadership is often compared to a grocery basket; in that, it is a collection of skills that must be cultivated and developed over time. Effective leaders must understand that their impact extends beyond their own actions and into the actions of those around them. They must possess the ability to communicate effectively, build relationships, and inspire others to achieve their goals.

Developing the skills and habits necessary for effective leadership takes time and effort. Leaders must be proactive in their development, seeking out opportunities for growth and continuously refining their skills. This process can be difficult and often requires a level of self-awareness and introspection, but the end result is a leader who is capable of driving meaningful change and inspiring those around them.

It is important to note that effective leadership requires a balance between the conscious, subconscious, and unconscious mind. Leaders must be mindful of their influence and the impact they have on those around them. They must avoid actions that are harmful or detrimental to their goals and instead strive to act in a manner that is consistent with their values and principles.

It requires time, effort, and self-reflection to develop, but the rewards are worth the investment. By embracing the principles of the conscious, subconscious, and unconscious mind, leaders can maximise their impact and create meaningful changes in the world around them.

Disclaimer:

In this book, all information about leadership discussed is based on Coach Fahad's personal experience, research, observations, and philosophical understandings over 21 years of corporate experience and more than ten years of experience in Human Resources and Leadership Development. It is important to note that these insights are not definitive and may not be suitable for every individual or organisation.

Leadership is a complex and multifaceted concept that is influenced by various factors such as habits, skills, and results. Coach Fahad believes that leadership is earned, not given,

and it takes time and effort to develop the skills and qualities necessary for effective leadership. Leadership is not just
about doing one's job well but also about the ability to influence others and be humanised in the process.

Coach Fahad views leadership as a collection of skills, much
like a grocery basket that must be filled with a variety of
items in order to be effective. Just as a grocery basket needs
to be filled with a variety of items, leaders need to possess
a range of skills and traits in order to be successful. These
skills may include things like communication, empathy, strategic thinking, and the ability to motivate others.

In addition to these skills, Coach Fahad also recognises the
importance of the conscious, subconscious, and unconscious
mind in leadership. These three aspects of the mind can have a
significant impact on a leader's behaviour and decision-making, and it is important for leaders to be aware of how these
different parts of their minds are influencing their actions.

Despite the insights and information provided in this book,
it is important to keep in mind that these are based on Coach
Fahad's personal experiences and understanding of the topic.
They may not be applicable to every individual or organisation
and should not be used as a substitute for professional advice.

The information provided in this book is meant to provide a
general overview of Coach Fahad's perspectives and experiences related to leadership development. However, it should
not be relied upon as a comprehensive guide, and it is rec-
ommended that individuals seek out additional resources
and professional advice to fully understand the complexities
of leadership.

ABOUT COACH FAHAD

Fahad Khalaf, also known as Coach Fahad, is a highly accomplished professional with over 21 years of corporate experience and over ten years of experience in HR and leadership development. Throughout his career, Fahad has worked in various regions such as Europe, Middle East, North Africa, and APAC, giving him a well-rounded understanding of the different cultural, economic, and business environments.

Coach Fahad is an accredited Master Coach by the International Authority of Professional Coaching and Mentoring, which demonstrates his expertise in coaching and mentoring. He is also a certified Psychometric Assessment tool Practitioner of Talent Acquisition and Employee Engagement, which further highlights his knowledge of tools and assessments that can aid in developing leadership skills and improving employee engagement.

In his role as a Subject Matter Expert, Fahad has been a committee member and consultant for various entities and administrations, offering his expertise and experience to help organisations grow and succeed. Throughout his career, Fahad has held leadership positions in different industries, including banking and financial institutions, travel, leisure and entertainment, eCommerce and digital marketing, business operations and customer experience, startups, and small and medium enterprises, where he has successfully overseen teams with headcounts of over 1,000 employees.

Fahad's accomplishments in his professional career are notable. He has increased employees' productivity by 14%, increased business performance by 9%, reduced turnover by 17%, and reduced operational costs by 8%, equating to a value of USD 381,000. He has also increased the employee engagement ratio of the workforce by 41% and reduced potential damage by USD 189,000.

As a coach and mentor, Fahad has conducted 57 coaching and mentoring sessions for stakeholders, leadership teams, and employees, with headcounts exceeding 1,000. He has also been instrumental in recruiting and placing over 127 candidates in the last three years, working independently and overseeing projects, which demonstrates his ability to manage talent acquisition and development programs effectively.

Additionally, Fahad has developed, managed, and facilitated over 84 training programs in the last three years, covering HR topics, soft skills, and people development, and has developed, managed, and overseen 11 Talent Management and Development programs. These programs have helped organisations develop their leadership skills and grow their businesses.

Fahad Khalaf (aka Coach Fahad) is a seasoned professional with a wealth of experience and expertise in HR and leadership development. His achievements and accomplishments speak to his ability to help organisations grow and succeed.